MAINLY HUMOROUS

Plays for secondary schools

MAINLY HUMOROUS
Plays for secondary schools

Edited by
Sadler, Hayllar, Powell

Illustrated by Bruce Baldwin

M

First published 1979 by
THE MACMILLAN COMPANY OF AUSTRALIA PTY LTD
107 Moray Street, South Melbourne 3205
5 Clarke Street, Crows Nest 2065
Reprinted 1980, 1981, 1982, 1983, 1984, 1985

Associated companies and representatives
throughout the world

National Library of Australia
cataloguing in publication data
Mainly humorous
ISBN 0 333 29888 8
    1. English drama. I. Sadler, Rex Kevin,
    joint ed. II. Hayllar, Thomas Albert S.,
    joint eed. III. Powell, Clifford J.,
    joint ed.
822'.008

Set in Baskerville and Helvetica by
The Markby Group, Melbourne
Printed in Hong Kong

Contents

Acknowledgements

The editors and publishers are grateful to the following for permission to reproduce copyright material:

Allan Mackay for *King Chicken* and *Sitting on Top of the World*, and Allan Mackay and Hodder & Stoughton (Australia) Limited for *Boots An' All;* Tom Hayllar for *The Pied Piper;* Cliff Powell for *The Origin of Roast Pig* and *Nutty News;* Evans Brothers Limited for *Red Hot Cinders* by Richard Tydeman; Lewis Gardner for *Werewolf in Town;* Larry Pigram for *Bonny Johnny, A Modern Romeo and Juliet* and *The Battle for Hopeless High;* Methuen & Co Ltd for 'The Raft' by Richard Parker from *Six Plays for Boys;* A. D. Peters & Co Ltd for the excerpt from *Noah* by André Obey.

Warning

Preface

Young actors like all kinds of plays, but what they love, above all, are humorous plays. Every student wants to have a part in a play, especially a humorous one that moves along at a fairly brisk pace. In this respect, all the plays in *Mainly Humorous* 'work' in the classroom.

Now for the first time students and teachers have a drama book exclusively devoted to humorous plays. Unlike the plays in other anthologies, these plays (written in the main by practising teachers) require very few props and can be performed script in hand at a moment's notice.

The plays have been chosen because of their entertainment and escapist potential.

On with the show!

King Chicken

Allan Mackay

Introduction

King Chicken is pure farce. It is often enough stated that farce is only worthwhile when it carries a moral message, that is when the laughter is directed against the more outrageous of man's activities and beliefs. Therefore one may be tempted to see in this play a comment on the white man abroad in 'unenlightened' countries. That may be so, but the play's main aim is one of simple humour through absurdity.

Every role should be overacted in the best traditions of farce, with every actor doing his best to upstage and out-act the rest of the cast, using grandiose movements of arms and legs and exaggerated tones of voice. They should also try to exaggerate the accents of the Englishmen and the natives, in this way adding much more to the comedy.

Cast

Bottomley }	English explorers
Stanley	
Jane	
Tarzan	
Chief of the Bantu Tribe	
Mongo	His second-in-command
Witchdoctor	
Doctor Livingstone	
Narda	The daughter of the Chief
Two Natives	

SCENE

Deepest Africa, last century. A jungle clearing with a big rock centre stage.
Bottomley *and* **Stanley** *are crouched behind the rock, looking fearfully off.*

Bottomley   End of the line for us, Stanley old friend, end of the line! Surrounded on all sides by a herd of raging elephants out for our good British blood!

Stanley   Buck up, Bottomley — we'll fight to the last bitter drop!

Bottomley   But how, man, how? Our guns are empty, you've sprained your ankle and I've caught jungle malaria that's slowly driving me insane. It's no use! We're finished! The last hunt!

Stanley   Bit of a tough spot, I must admit. Still, we can look on the bright side.

Bottomley   What bright side? We're trapped and there's no way out!

Stanley   I don't suppose we'll ever find Doctor Livingstone now. Six months we've been searching this cursed jungle, looking behind every tree, in every bush, under every stone, and now . . .

Bottomley   To finish our lives squashed flat under the foot of a charging elephant! What a horrible way to die — it's . . . it's so . . . un-British!

Stanley   Come, come, Bottomley, don't go to pieces.

Bottomley   A poor joke, old man, under the circumstances.

Stanley   Forgive me, my friend — just trying to cheer you up.

Bottomley   Cheer me up, he says! My heavens, how Myrtle will mourn for me! Ah, my dear wife . . . if only I could see her smiling face once more. And what of little Norton and tiny Matilda? Left — without a father! How heartbreaking —

Stanley   You can't give in, Bottomley. Remember that an Englishman never says die, never! It's simply not done! Whatever would they say about you back at the club?

Bottomley   What does it matter, Stanley? It's over! (*He looks off*). The elephants are coming closer, closer! I can hear the thunder of their charge! I can almost see the whites of their eyes!

Stanley   Then let us at least die like proud and brave sons of old England!

Bottomley   How?

Stanley   Screaming for mercy. Help! Someone! Anyone!

(**Jane** *comes bounding in. She is dressed in animal skins.*)

Jane   Hullo, big white bwanas.

Bottomley   Stanley, someone heard us!

Jane   Whole jungle hear you.

Stanley   Great Scott — it's a woman . . . I think.

Jane   Me Jane.

(*Both men rise and face her.*)

Stanley   How do you do, Miss . . . er . . . I'm sorry, I didn't catch the last name.

Jane   Me Jane. Me Tarzan's woman. You heard of Tarzan?

Bottomley   Tarzan? I don't believe it!

Jane   Why not? This only fairy tale. Anything possible.

Stanley   We're pleased to meet you, Mrs Tarzan. I'm Stanley, he's Bottomley —

Bottomley   Stanley, we've got no time for idle chatter! (*He spins around*). They're coming closer! I can hear the pounding of their feet, the panting of their breath —

Stanley   Shame, Bottomley — an Englishman should never forget his manners. Pardon me, Jane, but there's this dashed herd of elephants out yonder that's giving us quite a bit of bother. Nuisance really. Now, what can you do?

Jane   (*looking off*) Me do what Tarzan teach Jane to do.

Bottomley   What's that?

Jane   Get the heck out of here!

Bottomley   But how? We're surrounded!

Jane   Me swing through trees giving Tarzan's bloodcurdling yell.

Stanley   I've often wondered — why does he do that?

Jane   Me don't know, but it sure scare the daylights out of jungle.

Bottomley   Miss Jane, there aren't any trees here to swing through!

Jane   Oh oh! Jane better call Tarzan.

Stanley   That's the ticket! Imagine, the great Tarzan, in the flesh.

Jane   Not quite. Him wear loin cloth.

Bottomley   Stanley, there's no time for this! Let's make a run for it!

Stanley   Calm down, old chap — don't you get a kick out of meeting new people?

Bottomley   Not when I'm about to be hammered six feet into the ground!

(***Jane** has climbed up on the rock.*)

Stanley   Listen to this, Bottomley, the famous call of the jungle. See how she braces herself on that rock. See how she raises her cupped hands to her mouth. We're about to hear what no white man has ever heard —

Jane   (*shouting*) Tarzan! Leave dishes and get lazy self over here, quick smart!

Bottomley   I've heard that before, It's why I came to the jungle.

*(**Jane** climbs down off the rock. The distant sound of **Tarzan's** famous call is heard.)*

Stanley   There it is, the *real* call of the jungle!

Jane   No, that Tarzan falling off roof. There are no trees over there, either.

*(**Tarzan** enters, limping and bruised. He, too, is dressed in skins and has a knife strapped to his waist.)*

Tarzan   What happen to rotten trees? They there ten years ago.

Jane   Him not only clumsy, him not very bright. We in another part of the jungle ten years ago.

Tarzan   What you want, woman? Tarzan busy working on stamp collection.

Jane   Great white hunters in trouble.

Tarzan   Hullo, great white hunters. Me Tarzan, Lord of the Jungle! Me Tarzan the magnificent! Me Tarzan of the Apes!

Stanley   I don't see any apes.

Tarzan   Me just make that up when me saw you.

Bottomley   Humph! Off with you! An Englishman would rather be trampled than insulted.

Tarzan   Note Tarzan's beautiful body. Tarzan best swimmer in the world! Strongest man in the world! Fastest runner in the world! Second best wrestler in the world!

Stanley   Who's the best?

Tarzan   Jane. Tarzan a bit out of practice lately.

Jane   Tarzan live in very small world. Him really King of the Chickens but him got big head.

Tarzan   They pretty fierce chickens, woman!

Bottomley   Stanley — the elephants!

Stanley   Oh, yes, Tarzan, be a good chap and do something spectacular to save us from the elephants.

Tarzan   What you after — cheap thrill? How you expect me to do that?

Bottomley   But you said you were the King of the Jungle.

Tarzan   You know that, me know that, chickens know that. But me have lots of trouble lately convincing elephants.

Jane   And Jane.

Bottomley   Can't you do anything?

Tarzan   Why not use magic-stick-that-speak-with-thunder-and-lightning?

Stanley   What magic stick, old boy?

Tarzan   That point-four-four calibre elephant gun with telescopic sights.

Stanley   Empty, I'm afraid. Dashed nuisance, really.

Tarzan   Then us in one big mess.

Jane   Him just work that out. Told you him not very bright.

Bottomley   Can't you order them to go away? Don't you speak the language of all animals?

Tarzan   What language elephant speak?

Stanley   Better give it a try, Tarzan old thing. One good blast for the old school and all that.

Tarzan   Me try.

(He climbs up on the rock and cups his hands around his mouth. The others look eagerly off.)

Elephants, go home!

(There is a long pause.)

Stanley   They're not going.

Jane   Still hope. Maybe they die laughing.

Tarzan   Maybe they foreign elephants. We get many migrants this time of year.

Bottomley   Do something! They're almost on us!

Jane   Climb down, bigmouth. Jane try.

*(**Tarzan** climbs down and **Jane** clambers up on the rock.)*

Tarzan   Ha! What can silly woman do that Tarzan can't do?

Jane   *(shouting)* Elephants, go home or Jane come out there and give you good tongue lashing!

(There is a long pause.)

Stanley   *(peering off)* They're going.

Bottomley   Oh, man, look at them go.

Tarzan   Beginners' luck.

Bottomley   Incredible! We're saved! *(He laughs loudly.)*

Tarzan   What wrong with him? Did Tarzan make joke?

Jane   Tarzan one big joke.

(She climbs down.)

Stanley   I say, Jane, thanks a million. You saved our lives.

Jane   Save Jane's life, too, but me do the same for you even if me not here.

Stanley   However did you do it?

Jane   What work on Tarzan work on elephants.

Tarzan   No wonder me Tarzan of the Chickens.

Bottomley   Well, at least we can relax now, Stanley, and get back to the real business of our expedition.

Stanley   Indeed, yes. I say, Tarzan, have you heard of a fellow out here by the name of Livingstone?

Tarzan   Who he?

Stanley   A doctor.

Tarzan   Which doctor?

Stanley   No, white doctor, though you might call him a white witch-doctor — or is it a witch white doctor?

Tarzan   Tarzan all mixed up.

Jane   Tarzan back to normal then.

Stanley   Doctor Livingstone came to Africa two years ago to help the natives. But he disappeared.

Tarzan   If he disappear, how you find him?

Stanley   We must try. That's why we came here. The world must know that he's safe.

Jane   Jane hear of white doctor in Bantu village near here.

Stanley   By Jove, that could be him!

Jane   Him have much trouble with local witchdoctor. They fight all the time. Steal patients off each other. Have price war on medicines. Much bad blood.

(The sound of tom-toms is heard.)

Bottomley   Listen, Stanley — drums!

Tarzan   Nice tune. Bantus very musical tribe.

Bottomley   Are they dangerous?

Tarzan   Only to people. They cook people in pot.

Bottomley   Out of the fire and into the frying pan! Stanley, we're trapped again!

Tarzan White friends not worry. Natives afraid of Tarzan.

Jane White friends better worry.

Tarzan One look at Tarzan's face and natives run away.

Jane Jane often tempted herself.

(Enter the native chief and **Mongo**, *his second-in-command. They are dressed in grass skirts and carry spears.)*

Bottomley Cannibals!

*(***Bottomley*** and ***Stanley*** cower back.)*

Chief Hey, Mongo, look here — King Chicken himself. Stick him before him run away again!

Tarzan Bantu, stand back! Tarzan command!

Chief What him talking about?

Mongo Ah, him talk big without his chickens.

Chief For a swinger, him one big flop.

Mongo Me give him fast spear up belly button.

Tarzan Bantu, beware! Tarzan call all jungle friends to help him!

Chief Ha! Last time him do that, Bantu have to fight off two old rats and flea-bag monkey.

Jane Jane not even bother to come.

Chief We put him in cook pot with big fat doctor. Make a nice taste.

Mongo Add bit of body to stew.

Stanley *(stepping forward)* Wait! Did you say a doctor?

Chief You hear right.

Stanley Which doctor?

Chief No, white doctor.

Stanley Pardon me, I meant which white doctor?

Chief Oh, is white doctor witch doctor, too? Bantu witchdoctor not white doctor.

Tarzan Tarzan getting headache.

Stanley   What's the doctor's name?

Chief   Which doctor? White doctor or witchdoctor?

Stanley   White doctor. What's his name?

Chief   Big fat doctor. Me not catch last name. Who you, stranger?

Stanley   We're Englishmen.

Chief   You lucky, today's menu full or you in lots of trouble. You come back tomorrow?

Stanley   We'll be gone tomorrow and we'll be taking your victim with us. He's the famous Doctor Livingstone and we came all the way to Africa to find him.

Chief   Him must be real wild taste if you come that far.

Stanley   We don't want to eat him, we want to save him.

Chief   Too bad. Ever since white doctor come to village, Bantu have poor luck. Well dry up, animals go away, everyone get sick, Chief start to lose at poker —

Mongo   Even Chief's daughter sick in bed for three days. Sinking fast.

Chief   White doctor bring evil spirit to Bantu!

Mongo   Him die in cook pot!

Bottomley   But that's cold-blooded murder!

Mongo   Not cold. Bantu boil first. Bantu civilized natives.

Chief   Hot, cold — Chief too hungry to care. Chief hasn't had square meal since white missionary come to dinner. Now all invited to dinner! Plenty to go round! Witchdoctor, bring in food!

*(The last bit is shouted off. A few moments later the witchdoctor brings in **Livingstone** at the point of a spear. The witchdoctor is ceremoniously dressed in elaborate mask and robes.)*

Bottomley   Look, Stanley, it's Livingstone!

Stanley   By gad, so it is. What a lucky break!

Chief   Bring in pot!

(Two natives struggle in with a huge pot.)

Bottomley   Not so lucky for dear old Livingstone.

Stanley   We must save him.

Chief   White doctor get in pot!

Livingstone   How dare you, sir, how dare you! Do you know who I am?

Chief   Sorry, we not introduced. Chief never get formal with food.

Livingstone   I'm a white man and an Englishman!

Chief   Should be juicy.

Witchdoctor   How Chief like his dinner, boiled or deep fried?

Chief   Boiled. Him look like tough old bird. Put doctor in pot!

(The two natives force **Livingstone** *into the pot.)*

Witchdoctor   Bring water!

(The two natives run off. **Stanley** *and* **Bottomley** *approach the pot.)*

Stanley   Doctor Livingstone, I presume.

Livingstone   By George, it's Stanley — and just in time!

Stanley   Sorry, old thing, I'm not hungry.

Livingstone   That joke, sir, was in very bad taste.

Stanley   Sorry. I say, you are in a tough spot.

Livingstone   It's an outrage! How dare they do this to a subject of the Queen! Get me out of here!

Bottomley   How?

Livingstone   Show them the Union Jack.

Bottomley   Haven't got one.

Livingstone   Shame on you. Isn't that Tarzan?

Bottomley   Yes.

Livingstone   Get him to help.

(The two natives return and pour buckets of water into the pot.)

Stanley   Capital idea.

*(He goes over to **Tarzan** who has been trying not to be noticed by the busy natives.)*

I say, Tarzan, could you lend us a hand here?

Tarzan   Which one you want?

Jane   Both useless.

Stanley   Please try to save our friend.

Tarzan   Why should I?

Stanley   Because you're a white man like us.

Tarzan   You sure?

Stanley   Of course. It's obvious.

Tarzan   Fancy that. Me just thought me lightly sun-tanned native.

Stanley   No, true blue white.

Jane   Jane, too?

Stanley   Certainly.

Tarzan   I say, how simply smashing! Not to worry, white brothers, Tarzan have you out of mess in two ticks.

Livingstone   Good show!

Jane   Jane not like. Jane prefer natives.

*(**Tarzan** goes over to the **Chief**.)*

Tarzan   Pardon me, Chiefy old thing, how would you like to free my friends here?

Chief   How you like sudden spear up white snoot?

Tarzan   Oh, I say, Chiefy, that's not very sporting.

Chief   Get wood for fire!

*(The two natives go out. Meanwhile, the witchdoctor has approached **Jane**.)*

Witchdoctor   We about to cook. Hey, what part you want, Jane baby?

Jane   What part you got, big boy?

Witchdoctor   Slice of shoulder, leg —

Jane   Me have what you have, handsome.

Witchdoctor   Hey, you some dish yourself. How you get stuck with old fairy-feet over there?

Jane   Jane just silly young girl then. Got swept off feet.

Tarzan   Jane, come away from that savage.

Witchdoctor   Who you call savage? You just big noise in trees.

Tarzan   Tarzan strongest white man in world!

Witchdoctor   Tarzan out of this world.

Stanley   Chief, you must let Livingstone go.

Chief   What you trying to do, take food out of our mouths? Tribe must eat.

(The two natives return and heap wood around the pot.)

Bottomley   But you can't cook him!

Chief   Why not? We got good recipe.

Stanley   He's an Englishman!

Chief   Still taste the same.

Stanley   But he's a white man!

Chief That only make him a bit hard to stomach. Get fire!

Livingstone No, no — save me!

> *(The two natives are about to go out when Princess Narda strides in.)*

Narda Father, stop!

Mongo Look, it Princess Narda!

Chief Daughter, you not sick. Evil spirits gone.

Narda Me saved by magic medicine of white doctor.

Chief Chief thank great white doctor. Take him from cooking pot!

> *(The two natives help Livingstone out of the pot.)*

Livingstone Saved, saved!

Chief Chief make you honorary member of Bantu tribe.

Livingstone I say, what a good idea. They'll never believe this back at the club.

Chief It tribal law that man who save daughter of chief, marry her.

Narda Ooooooh, daddy. At last Narda get pretty husband all her own. Love him like crazy.

Chief Hey, white doctor, what you doing?

Livingstone Getting back into the pot.

Chief Chief has spoken. We prepare wedding feast.

Livingstone Mercy, mercy!

Chief Chief also make two white hunters members of tribe. You now Bantu.

Stanley Splendid!

Bottomley Marvellous!

Tarzan Suddenly Tarzan only white man around.

Witchdoctor But Chief, now larder empty. How can we have wedding feast?

> *(Jane whispers in the Chief's ear.)*

Tarzan *(to Livingstone)* Tarzan glad he white man. Now go back to England, become king.

Chief *(to Jane)* Good idea. Then you marry witchdoctor. Kill two birds with one stone.

Tarzan Why everyone look at Tarzan? Tarzan getting funny feeling he in lots of trouble . . .

(The two natives grab Tarzan.)

Tarzan No, no! Natives not cook Tarzan! Tarzan white man!

Chief Big deal.

Tarzan Jane, save Tarzan!

Jane Who Tarzan? Tarzan only made up in book.

Tarzan White brothers, save Tarzan!

Stanley Sorry. We natives.

Bottomley Me can't stand white man.

Chief Come, Bantu go home. Cook in comfort, eat in comfort.

(Exit struggling Tarzan, witchdoctor, Jane and natives.)

Come, new son-in-law.

Livingstone Just let me say goodbye to my friends.

Narda Husband not be long. Narda go to make herself look pretty for wedding. Put snake oil on hair, put on wedding dress of hyena skin, paint nails with monkey blood. Look very beautiful.

(Exit the Chief and Narda.)

Livingstone Stanley, we've got to get out of here!

Stanley But you're engaged to be married.

Bottomley Lovely girl — look beautiful.

Livingstone Then *you* marry her.

Bottomley Let's make a run for it. This way!

(They are about to leave when they are stopped by the distant sound of Tarzan's call.)

Stanley Wait! Listen to that! At last, at long last, the famous call of the jungle! Tarzan the Magnificent!

Bottomley King of the Chickens!

Stanley   Lord of the Jungle!

Livingstone   Gone to pot!

*(**Tarzan's** call is heard again but this time it is much louder, suggesting a sticky end. It finally fades into a gurgle. The three explorers hurry out.)*

CURTAIN

Questions

1 Why do you think the play is called 'King Chicken'?

2 Who are Stanley and Bottomley looking for in the jungles of deepest Africa, and how long have they been at it?

3 Quote a line or two to show that Jane does not think much of Tarzan's mental abilities.

4 Energy and leadership are both qualities possessed by the 'real' Tarzan of the Apes. How does the Tarzan of 'King Chicken' measure up?

5 One form of humour used in the play is the pun or play on words. Example: 'To finish our lives squashed flat under the foot of a charging elephant . . .' 'Come, come, Bottomley, don't go to pieces.'
   Give two more examples of puns from the play.

6 Show your particular knowledge of the play by finishing Tarzan's descriptions of himself:
   'Me Tarzan Lord ....'
   'Me Tarzan the ....,'
   'Me Tarzan of ....'
And now finish off what others say about him:
   'Him really .... but him got ....'
   'For a swinger him ....'
   'How you get stuck with .... over there?'

7 How has Dr Livingstone made himself unpopular in the Bantu village?

8 The Chief of the Bantus has a single-minded interest in people. What does he see in them?

9 Why does Jane finally desert Tarzan?

10 Explain how poor Tarzan is finally lured into the cooking pot towards the end of the play.

The Pied Piper

Tom Hayllar
*(Adapted from the poem
by Robert Browning)*

Cast

Pied Piper
Narrator
Frau Hof
Frau Hip   } Three Housewives
Frau Finkel
Mayor
First Councillor
Second Councillor
Third Councillor
Cleaning Lady
Office Boy
Willy
First Man
Second Man
Third Man

Narrator   The place is Hamelin Town, in Brunswick Germany, near the River Weser. The year is 1376, also known as the Year of the Rat, for reasons that will become only too obvious as we listen in to a typical conversation in a Hamelin street . . .

Frau Hof   In my bed! I found a rat in my own bed!

Frau Hip   No . . . Not in your bed?

Frau Hof   Ja! Listen to me, it's getting so that I can't stand them any more. There are thousands and thousands of them.

Frau Hip   Millions of them.

Frau Hof   Exactly. Listen! There are so many they have scared off all the dogs. No dog with half a brain is going to live in *this* town.

Frau Hip   Ja. And I have just been saying to my Ludwig who used to have such an excellent sense of smell till a rat bit him on the nose and . . . and . . . Where was I?

Frau Hof   You were saying to your Ludwig.

Frau Hip   Oh, ja. I was saying to my Ludwig that once it was the cats who used to chase the rats. Now it's the other way round and there are cats running for their lives from the rats everywhere.

Frau Hof   Speak up, Frau Hip, I can't hear what you're saying above all the squeaking and shrieking from the rats.

Frau Hip   I said 'RATS EVERYWHERE'!

Frau Hof   Oh, ja. Even in my kitchen. Yesterday, just as I was lifting the ladle to taste the soup, out sprang two rats and slurped it up before I could get the ladle to my mouth!

Frau Hip   That's nothing. When my Ludwig went to put on his best hat for church, last Sunday, out fell a rat's nest. Ugh! You should have seen them — big, grey brutes with scaly tails and long claws, running all over his bald patch, nibbling his moustache, hanging onto his ears, and poor Ludwig, he nearly screamed the roof off . . . and I don't blame him.

Frau Finkel *(Rushing from a doorway)* A rat has just bitten my baby!

Frau Hof Where?

Frau Finkel On the ear.

Frau Hof Tie it off at the neck.

Frau Finkel I'll tie you off at the neck, Frau Hof, if you're not careful!

Frau Hip Ladies, save your abuse for the rats. It's either them or us.

Frau Hof Somebody has *got* to *do* something.

Frau Hip It's a job for the Mayor.

Frau Hof Exactly. Let *him* do the dirty work.

Frau Finkel Ja, ja. We pay taxes to keep the Mayor and the rest of the Councillors in office, don't we? So isn't it only fair that he and his Councillors should earn their keep and rid us of the rats?

Frau Hof Of course it is. Come on then, ladies. Let's get our husbands and the rest of the townspeople and march to the Town Hall. We'll tell the Mayor and the Councillors to get on with the job if they want to keep their jobs.

Narrator So, a crowd of townsfolk, gathering strength as it went, marched to the Town Hall and stood outside it chanting 'Rid us of the rats' until the Lord Mayor was forced to admit three people who happened to be the three housewives . . .

IN THE TOWN HALL

Mayor *(To **Frau Hof**)* What is it then? Speak up, my good woman. I haven't got all day . . . my time's valuable you know. What is it?

Frau Hof It's the rats, your honour. Get rid of them or we'll get rid of you!

Mayor Now just a minute, my good woman . . .

Frau Hip   Don't give us that 'good woman' rubbish. Either get rid of the rats or we'll have you out of office in a flash!

Frau Finkel   On your ear!

Mayor   How dare you speak to me like that! It's an insult to my robes and chains of office. *(Turning)* Councillors!

Councillors   Yes, Mr Mayor?

Mayor   Throw these loud-mouthed hussies down the Town Hall steps and be quick about it.

Frau Hof   *(Rolling up her sleeves)* The first person who lays hands on me will have his ears boxed.

   *(The **Councillors** retire nervously.)*

   I've come here to talk to you about —

All Women   Rats!

Frau Hof   They fight the dogs

Frau Hip   And kill the cats.

Frau Finkel   And bite the babies in their cradles.

Frau Hof   And eat the cheeses out of the vats. And lick the soup from the cook's own ladles.

Frau Hip   Make nests inside men's Sunday hats.

Frau Finkel   Split open the kegs of salted sprats.

Frau Hof   And spoil the women's chats
By drowning their speaking
With shrieking and squeaking
In fifty different sharps and flats.

Frau Finkel   And what are you going to do about it?

Mayor   I can't think . . . I mean, I will immediately review the matter.

(More of the crowd forces its way in through the door . . .)

First Man   It seems as though our mayor is a bit of a fool.

Mayor   I wouldn't say that, my man, I . . .

Second Man   Well, you must be if you haven't found a way of getting rid of all these rats by now.

Third Man   We can't put up with them any longer.

First Man   And, what's more we're sick and tired of the excuses of you and your Councillors. We're fed up with all your talk. We want to see a bit of action around here.

Frau Hof   So make up your minds quick and lively.

Frau Hip   We'll give you twenty-four hours to get rid of all the rats in town. *(Exit the townspeople.)*

Mayor   Well, that settles it. We'll have to come up with something or our life of ease will be finished.

First Councillor   But we've tried everything we know to get rid of the rats.

Mayor   *(Angrily)* Shut your trap! *(Snaps his fingers)* Which reminds me. Who tested the new economy size *Gotcha* rat trap we bought yesterday?

Second Councillor   *(Unhappily)* I did, Mr Mayor.

Mayor   *(Snapping his fingers.)* Come on, man . . . the results?

Second Councillor   Well, my wife and I set it up in the middle of the kitchen floor with at least half a kilo of the ripest Gorgonzola . . .

First Councillor   Phewww!

Mayor   Be quiet! Proceed, Councillor.

Second Councillor   Yes, well, as I was saying before the somewhat rude interruption . . .

Mayor   Get on with it!

Second Councillor   *(Hastily)* Next morning there were all the rats. . .

All   *(Excitedly)* In the trap?

Mayor   Great heavens. Nothing's going to stop me bestowing the Lord Mayor's Gold Medal on this fellow right away.

Second Councillor   *(Sadly)* No, not *in* the trap. All the rats were sitting in a circle *round* the trap killing themselves laughing.

Mayor   Silence! This is no laughing matter.

   (Turning to the **Third Councillor***).*

   Well, what about that rat poison you were going to use — 'rat' something or other?

Third Councillor   *Ratoff*, your Honour.

Mayor   That's the stuff. Guaranteed to er. . .

Third Councillor   To rack off all rats, your Honour.

Mayor   Yes, of course. Well, now, how did it go?

Third Councillor   Not so good, your Honour. Instead of racking them off, it turned them on. I found old Ronny unscrewing the cork with his tail and swigging it down when he thought I wasn't looking.

Mayor   Ronny?

Third Councillor   Ronny the rat, your Worship. He's kind of the leader of the pack. But then there's Ralph, and Rocky and Rudolph.

Mayor *(Gasping)* You must be joking.

Third Councillor   Oh no, your Honour . . . We . . . that is my good wife and I . . . We've grown to love all our rats. All of them have their own little names and if one of them gets sickly — bless its little whiskers — we feed it with *Ratoff* till it gets better. Take poor little Ricky, real weedy she was, till we gave her daily doses of *Ratoff* and now she's as robust a rodent as ever riddled a cheese.

Mayor   *(Weakly)* Someone get Doctor Quakov, the Councillor has gone ratty . . . I mean nutty. What else have we done? *(Appealing)* We must have done something else to get rid of this plague?

First Councillor   We've tried blocking their holes, but as fast as we block them up, they make new ones.

Second Councillor   And we've tried to burn them out, but only succeed in burning down our own houses!

Mayor   *(Groaning)* I give up. We've done everything. I'm ready to resign. It's easy for the townspeople to say 'solve the rat problem', but my head's spinning so much that even the word 'rat' gives me a big, ugly headache with a tail.

First Councillor   It's all quite hopeless . . . We'll *never* get rid of the rats.

(There is a knock at the door)

Mayor What's that?

Second Councillor Probably some large rat scraping its feet on the mat.

Mayor Anything like the sound of a rat makes my heart miss a beat.

Narrator The sound of another knock is heard on the door.

Mayor Come in!

Narrator And in did come the strangest figure!
    His queer long coat, from heel to head
    Was half of yellow and half of red;
    And he himself was tall and thin,
    With sharp blue eyes, each like a pin,
    And loose light hair, yet swarthy skin,
    No tuft on cheek nor beard on chin,
    But lips where smiles went out and in;
    There was no guessing his kith and kin.
    And nobody could enough admire
    The tall man and his quaint attire.

Mayor Who . . . Who are you?

First Councillor *(Amazed)* He's the oddest looking fellow I've ever seen.

Second Councillor *(Admiringly)* What a marvellous outfit he's wearing.

Third Councillor *(In wonder)* His clothes seem to glow with colour.

First Councillor Notice his fingers keep fiddling with that musical pipe he's got hung around his neck, as if he wants to put it to his lips and play it right this instant.

Mayor Come, come, my good man, don't stand there. We haven't got all year, you know. State your business and be off.

Pied Piper If it please your Honours. I can rid your town forever of the rats.

Mayor and Councillors Impossible!

Mayor   What kind of madness is this? How can *you* succeed where we have failed? I mean . . . been unsuccessful to date?

Pied Piper   Your Honours, I am able
By means of a secret charm, to draw
All creatures living beneath the sun,
That creep, or swim, or fly, or run,
After me, so as you never saw.
And I chiefly use my charm
On creatures that do people harm,
On mole and toad, and newt, and viper,
And people call me the Pied Piper.

Mayor   Proof! Give me proof of these claims.

Pied Piper   Well poor piper as I am,
In Tartary I freed the Cham
Last June, from his huge swarms of gnats,
I eased in Asia the Nizam
Of a monstrous brood of vampire bats.

Mayor   You did all that?

Pied Piper   I did.

Mayor   You're hired on the spot!

Pied Piper   I'll rid your town of the rats all right but my fee is one thousand guilders.

Mayor   A paltry one thousand guilders? Listen my man, if you can rid this town of its rat plague, we'll give you fifty thousand guilders. *(Turning to the **Councillors**)* Won't we?

Councillors   My word, we will. Willingly. Cash as soon as the job's done.

Pied Piper   Well, your Honours, if you'll excuse me, I'll get on with it at once . . .

Narrator   Into the street the Piper stept
Smiling first a little smile,
As if he knew what magic slept
In his quiet pipe the while;
Then, like a musical adept,
To blow the pipe his lips he wrinkled,
And green and blue his sharp eyes twinkled,
Like a candle-flame where salt is sprinkled;
And ere three shrill notes the pipe uttered,
You heard as if an army muttered;
And the muttering grew to a grumbling;
And the grumbling grew to a mighty rumbling;
And out of the houses the rats came tumbling.

(IN THE TOWN HALL)

Mayor   There's something decidedly odd about that fellow.

First Councillor   Rather piercing eyes, I thought.

Mayor   I hope we've done the right thing . . .

Office Boy   *(At the window)* Look Mr Mayor . . . There goes the Piped Piper playing his flute and skipping down the street.

Mayor   What's that? *(Rushing to the window)* Let me see.

Cleaning Lady   Listen, there's some other sound. Ooh, I'm a bit scared.

Office Boy   It's quite like thunder, isn't it?

Cleaning Lady   Ooooh . . . Look over there.

Mayor   Where? I can't see anything.

Cleaning Lady   There . . . and there. From all the doorways.

Mayor   Rats! Great heavens, they're pouring out into the street like a flood!

Office Boy   And they're all following the Pied Piper.

First Councillor   I can't believe my eyes!

Third Councillor   There goes little Ricky. Racing to the front. (*Proudly*) It's the *Ratoff* that does it.

(DOWN IN THE STREET)

Frau Hof   Great rats, small rats, lean rats, brawny rats,

Frau Hip   Brown rats, black rats, grey rats, tawny rats,

Frau Finkel   Grave old plodders, gay young friskers, Fathers, mother, uncles, cousins,

First Man   Cocking tails, and pricking whiskers,

Second Man   Families by tens and dozens;

Third Man   Brothers, sisters, husbands, wives —
Following the Piper for their lives.

(UP IN THE TOWN HALL)

Mayor   Just look at him go. Piping up and down the street with his cheeks bulging fit to bust.

Cleaning Lady   Ooh, and just look at the rats. There must be thousands of them just following him wherever he goes.

Office Boy   That flute of his must be magic.

(DOWN IN THE STREET)

Frau Hof   What's he doing now?

Fray Hip   He's going towards the river.

Frau Finkel   With all the rats following him.

Frau Hof   Into the river! Look at that. They're all plunging in.

Frau Hip   What a commotion . . . some of them are trying to swim, but they're sinking.

Frau Finkel   They're all drowning . . . drowning.

Frau Hof   The water's still. They're all gone.

Frau Hip   No more rats!

Frau Finkel   Hamelin is rat free at last!

Narrator   You should have heard the Hamelin people.
Ringing the bells till they rocked the steeple.

Mayor   *(Leaning out of the Town Hall window)*

Poke out the nests, and block up the holes!
Consult with carpenters and builders,
And leave in our town not even a trace
Of the rats!

Narrator   Suddenly the Piper appeared in the market place. . .

Pied Piper   *(Calling up to the* **Mayor***):* The job is done. Now may I have my thousand guilders please?

First Councillor   With half that amount we could stock our Town Hall cellar with the best wines money can buy.

Second Councillor   It would be absolutely stupid,
To pay this sum to a wandering fellow,
With a gipsy coat of red and yellow!

Mayor   *(Winking)* Besides . . .
Our business was done at the river's brink;
We saw with our eyes the vermin sink,
And what's dead can't come to life, I think.

(Poking his head out the window)

Listen, Friend . . .
We're not the folks to shrink
From the duty of giving you something for drink
And a matter of money to put in your poke;
But, as for the guilders, what we spoke
Of them, as you very well know, was in joke.
Beside, our losses have made us thrifty.
A thousand guilders! come, take fifty!

Pied Piper   Listen, your Honour, I'm warning you once and for all.
Keep your side of the bargain and pay up . . . or else . . .
Folks who put me in a passion
May find me pipe to another fashion.

Mayor   *(Angrily)* How d'ye think I'll brook
Being worse treated than a cook?
Insulted by a lazy ribald
With idle pipe and vesture piebald!
You threaten us, fellow! Do your worst!
Blow your pipe there till you burst!

(The Pied Piper quietly departs)

First Councillor   Ha, that's got rid of that tricky scoundrel with his ridiculous flute. *(Leaning out of the window)* There he goes. *(Yells)* Good riddance!

Narrator   But although they might have finished with the Pied Piper, *he* hadn't finished with them . . .
Once more he stept into the street
And to his lips again
Laid his long pipe of smooth, straight cane;

Office Boy   *(At the window)* Look at him!

Mayor   What? What are you talking about, boy?

Office Boy   Look . . . he's putting his flute to his lips. He's beginning to play again.

Mayor   Ha! That won't do him much good.

Cleaning Lady   Ooh! Look at all the little children. They're rushing out of all the houses, just like the rats.

Mayor   What's that rustling noise?

Narrator   There was a rustling that seemed like a bustling
Of merry crowds justling at pitching and hustling
Small feeet were pattering, wooden shoes clattering
Little hands clapping and little tongues chattering
And, like fowls in a farmyard when barley is scattering,
Out came the children running.

(DOWN IN THE STREET)

Frau Hof   The children are all skipping along after the Piper

Frau Hip   Stop them! Stop them!

Frau Finkel   *(Trying to catch the children.)* Come here! Take my hand, please.

Frau Hof   It's no use! They can't hear you. They are hypnotized by his music.

Frau Hip   *(In tears)* All the little boys and girls,
With rosy cheeks and flaxen curls,

Frau Hof   And sparkling eyes and teeth like pearls,

Frau Finkel   Tripping and skipping run merrily after
The wonderful music with shouting and laughter.
Why doesn't the Mayor *do* something?

(UP IN THE TOWN HALL)

Mayor   *(To First Councillor)* What can we do? Offer him the thousand
guilders! Anything. Speak up man!

First Councillor   I - I - don't know. I think it's too late.

Narrator   The Mayor was dumb, and the Council stood
As if they were changed into blocks of wood,
Unable to move a step, or cry
To the children merrily skipping by
— And could only follow with the eye
That joyous crowd at the Piper's back.

Mayor   *(Groaning)* Oh, no! I can't bear to look!

(Covers his face with his hands.)

Cleaning Lady   He's going down the High Street . . . Wait a minute
— he's leading them all down to the river. *(Hushed voice)* Just
like the rats.

Mayor   *(Despairing)* What did I do to deserve this?

First Councillor   *(Groaning)* Our jobs won't be worth a fig when the
townspeople see the children follow the rats into the river.

Narrator   And now the Mayor was on the rack.
And the wretched Council's bosoms beat.
As the Piper turned from the High Street
To where the Weser rolled its waters
Right in the way of their sons and daughters.

Office Boy   *(Excitedly)* He's going towards the river. He's getting
closer. Wait! He's turned aside. Now he's leading all the children towards Koppelberg Hill.

Mayor   What? Where? *(Pushing the **office boy** aside)* Let me look, boy.
(Sighing with relief) Heaven be praised . . . so he is.

First Councillor   *(Gleefully)* Now we've got him!

Mayor   How do you mean?

First Councillor   Well, he can't get through Koppelberg Hill, can he?

Mayor   It's solid granite!

First Councillor   Right. So, as soon as he gets to the cliff face, he'll
have to stop fluting and carrying on.

Mayor   The children will break off and come back.

First Councillor   And then?

Mayor   We arrest him!

(They slap each other joyfully on the back)

(DOWN IN THE STREET)

Frau Hof   He can't get through the mountain so . . .

Frau Hip   We're going to get our children back!

Frau Finkel   Hooray!

First Man   Wait! The Piper has just reached the cliff face and . . .

Second Man   It's unbelievable.

Third Man   Something's happening to the mountain itself . . . a kind of door.

Narrator   As they reached the mountain-side,
A wondrous door opened wide,
As if a cavern was suddenly hollowed;
And the Piper advanced, and the children followed,
And when all were in to the very last,
The door in the mountainside shut fast.

Frau Finkel   *(Wailing)* All of them gone.

Frau Hof   Ja. He led them into the mountain which closed up behind them and poof! All were gone.

Frau Hip   No! Look! One child is left. My own little Willy! *(She rushes and hugs him)*. Tell us what happened, Willy.

Frau Hof   *(To **Willy**)* Listen to me. What made you all follow him so blindly?

Frau Finkel   Just like the rats.

Frau Hof   Ja. And right into the mountain?

Frau Hip   What did he promise you?

Willy   The Piper promised all the children — and me too . . . *(Sobbing)*
          To lead us to a joyous land,
          Joining the town and just at hand,
          Where waters gushed and fruit trees grew,
          And flowers put forth a fairer hue,
          And everything was strange and new;
          The sparrows were brighter than peacocks here,
          And their dogs outran our fallow-deer,
          And honey-bees had lost their stings,
          And horses were born with eagles' wings:
          And just as I became assured
          My lame foot would be speedily cured,
          The music stopped, and I stood still
          And found myself outside the hill,
          Left alone against my will,
          To go now limping as before,
          And never hear of that country more!

(WEEKS LATER – UP IN THE TOWN HALL)

Mayor   *(Sadly)* Well, gentlemen, I believe we've done everything humanly possible to satisfy the townspeople.

First Councillor   Yes, Mr Mayor. Letters have been sent out north, south, east and west, asking for news of the Pied Piper and the children.

Second Councillor   And promising a very generous reward.

Third Councillor   But no replies have been forthcoming.

Mayor   Therefore, as a mark of respect to that lost generation, I propose that we rename High Street, Pied Piper Street. I further propose that flute playing be banned forever in that fateful street.

First Councillor   May I also suggest, your Honour, that we set up a more permanent memorial to our lost children.

Second Councillor   Something like a stone inscribed with the story,
right where the cavern opened up.

Third Councillor   And may *I* suggest a special window in the church?

Mayor   We'll do it! Put aside a thousand guilders to pay for all this.
Nothing's too good if it will remind us of the day the Pied Piper
went to work in this town.

All Councillors   Amen.

Narrator   Oposite the place of the cavern
They wrote the story on a column
And on the great church-window painted
The same to make the world acquainted
How their children were stolen away;
And there it stands to this very day.
And I must not omit to say
That in Transylvania there's a tribe
Of alien people that ascribe
The outlandish ways and dress
On which their neighbours lay such stress
To their fathers and mothers having risen
Out of some subterranean prison
Into which they were trepanned
Long time ago in a mighty band,
Out of Hamelin town in Brunswick land,
But how or why, they don't understand.
Now, the moral of this story is as follows:

Mayor   Dear Friends,
Let you and me be wipers
Of scores out with all men — especially pipers!
And, whether they pipe us free from rats or from mice,
If we've promised them aught, let us keep our promise!

Questions

1 Do you think the housewives were right in complaining to the mayor about the rats? Why?

2 What effect did *Ratoff* have on little Ricky?

3 What was unusual about the Pied Piper's appearance?

4 What proof did the Pied Piper give of his ability at ridding people of creatures that did them harm?

5 Describe how the Pied Piper got rid of Hamelin's rats.

6 If you had been the mayor of Hamelin, what would you have done to get rid of the rats?

7 Why did all the children follow the Pied Piper?

8 Why didn't Willy disappear with the other children?

9 Do you agree with the Pied Piper's action in taking away Hamelin's children? Why?

10 What problems would there be in staging *The Pied Piper*?

The Origin of Roast Pig

Clifford Powell

Introduction

The Origin of Roast Pig, *based on Charles Lamb's essay, depicts the supposed Eastern origin of a favourite Western dish.*

Cast
Stage Manager
Bo-bo
Ho-ti
Court Attendant
Judge
Ho-wong
Juryman I
Juryman II

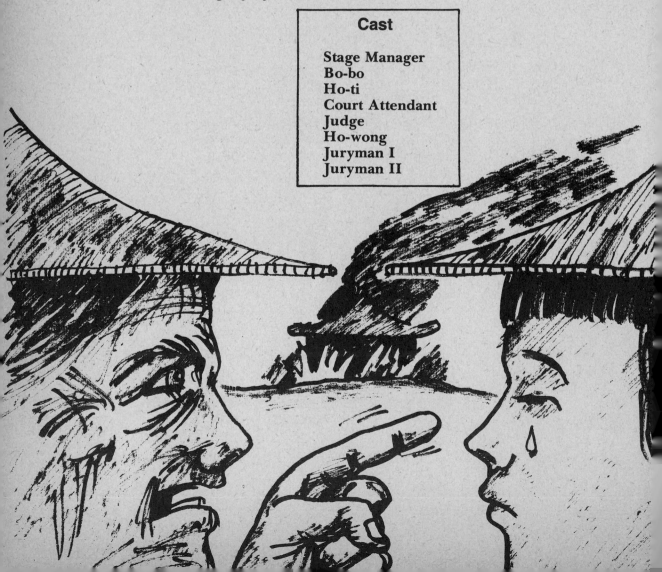

Stage Manager   I suppose the origins of many of the things we enjoy today would make an interesting story. We don't have time to look at a lot of these. But we're going to look at just one — quite a humorous affair it was. The origin of roast pig. Thousands of years ago in China a swineherd named Ho-ti lived with his son, Bo-bo. One day when Ho-ti was away Bo-bo accidentally set the house on fire. Here's what happened. *(He walks off. On come **Bo-bo** and **Ho-ti**.)*

SCENE I

Bo-bo   Father! Come quickly! The house is on fire.

Ho-ti   Oh, you foolish boy. Look at my house. How many times have I told you to keep away from the fire?

Bo-bo   But it was an accident, honourable father. I was just tending the fire when the wind blew some sparks out and before I knew what had happened the house was burning.

Ho-ti   You wicked boy. This is not the first time that you have burnt my house. An accident was it? Is this how you repay me for my goodness to you? Take that! *(He hits **Bo-bo**.)* Perhaps that will teach you to be more careful.

Bo-bo   Oh! Oh!

Ho-ti   But beating you does not bring my house back. More important it does not bring my pigs back. Oh, you are an ungrateful son!

Bo-bo   Oh, my father, all that you say is true. But I had forgotten about the pigs. The new litter of pigs will all be burnt! Is there nothing we can do?

Ho-ti   There is nothing to be done. A new house can be built with little labour but no amount of work can bring back pigs.

Bo-bo   *(sniffing the air)* Mmm! Honourable father, can you smell that delicious smell? It seems to come from the house.

Ho-ti   You imagine things. There is no smell but the smell of burning house.

Bo-bo   No, honourable father, this is such a smell as I have never detected before. It must be the burnt pigs. I will have a look.

(He goes offstage.)

Ho-ti Be careful or you will burn yourself.

Bo-bo *(Offstage)* I cannot see anything. Wait . . . Here is a little pig that has been burnt. *(He comes onstage with the piglet.)*

Ho-ti Here, let me see.

Bo-bo It is very burnt, honourable father, but there is no doubt this was a young pig. *(He turns it over.)* Ooo! Oww! I've burnt my fingers.

Ho-ti Put them in your mouth. That will take the pain away.

Bo-bo Ooo. Mmm. Mmmm!

Ho-ti And what is the matter now?

Bo-bo My fingers . . . Mmmm . . . They taste wonderful.

Ho-ti Oh, that I should be burdened with such a graceless son. First he burns down my house and now he says that his fingers taste wonderful!

Bo-bo But father, they do! It must be the pig. *(He touches the pig again and puts his fingers in his mouth.)* Mmmm! Mmmm!

Ho-ti Stop it at once I say, you offensive boy! Give that to me. *(He takes the pig off **Bo-bo**.)* Oh, it's hot still. Ooo! I've burnt myself.

Bo-bo Put your fingers in your mouth, father.

Ho-ti Ooo! Mmmm! Mmmmm! It certainly does taste wonderful. Here, let me taste it again. *(They keep touching the pig and putting their fingers in their mouths.)*

Bo-bo To think that never before had we tasted burnt pig. It truly is a marvellous taste.

Ho-ti But we must not allow the rest of the people to know. They would think that we were thankless creatures to spoil the natural taste of meat that the gods send us.

Bo-bo Then we will be the only ones who will know the succulent taste of burnt pig. If others find out they will take us before the judges.

Ho-ti Yes, and they will have us put to death. We must be careful. We will build another house and buy another pig and when she has a litter, you will accidentally set fire to the house . . . and . . .

Bo-bo And we will have more roast pig. Oh, honourable father, that is a clever idea. Here, father, have some more roast pig. Mmmm! *(They walk off.)*

SCENE II

Stage Manager The two continued their houseburning as often as they could get a litter of pigs. But the neighbours began to notice that Ho-ti's house was being burnt down just a little too often for it to be an accident. Then someone noticed that there was always a litter of pigs in the house when it was burnt. Finally the neighbours set themselves to watch and, sure enough, they caught Ho-ti and Bo-bo tasting burnt pig. As they had feared. Ho-ti and Bo-bo were summoned to appear in Pekin, to be tried by the High Court of China.

Court Attendant The court is to come to silence! *(A gong is struck.)* Stand for the High Court Judge!

Judge The court may be seated. Proceed with the case.

Attendant Your Honour, the case of Ho-ti and Bo-bo, accused before the court this day of having committed an outrageous crime. It is said that they ate burnt pig!

Judge   Call the first witness.

Ho-wong   Your Honour, I am here.

Judge   You will tell the court your name and the facts of this case that you know.

Ho-wong   My name is Ho-wong. Your Honour, for several years now, I and my fellow neighbours have noticed that the house of Ho-ti has been burnt down an unusual number of times. That would make a normal man very angry.

Judge   You speak with sound reason.

Ho-wong   Not only has the house been burnt many times, your Honour, but on each occasion it has contained a litter of young pigs. Now to lose them would make a normal person very angry. But Ho-ti did not seem at all angry. In fact, your Honour, he seemed pleased.

Judge   Is this true, Ho-ti?

Ho-ti   Yes, your Honour. Ho-wong tells the truth.

Judge   Continue your story, Ho-wong.

Ho-wong   At last I and my fellow neighbours, being concerned for the good of our friend Ho-ti, watched him carefully and we saw him set fire to his own house. Then he took of the burnt pigs that were inside and ate. And not only that but he gave to his son to eat. And, greater disgrace, the two of them seemed to enjoy it.

Judge   Really this is the most disgraceful accusation that I have ever heard. It seems quite clear that the accused are guilty of this vile offence. What does the jury think?

Juryman I   Your Honour, we feel that the case is clear, too. However, we would like to see some of this offensive burnt pig.

Judge   Attendant, is there any of this repulsive roast pig to be exhibited?

Attendant   Your Honour, I have sent for my house to be burnt down . . . with a pig in it.

Judge   Ahh, an excellent piece of thinking.

Attendant   Here comes the burnt pig now.

Judge   Take it across to the jury.

Juryman I   See how repulsive it looks. This is clearly dishonouring to the gods who have given us good, wholesome, raw meat for food. Here, let me see it. Ohh. Oooo! I've burnt myself.

Ho-ti   Put your fingers in your mouth.

Juryman I   Owww! Mmmm! Beautiful. Here, let me try some more. Mmmmmm!

Juryman II   Let me see the burnt pig. Mmm, it is delicious!

Judge   Gentlemen, have you forgotten yourselves? Attendant, take the exhibit from them and bring it here. Now, let me see. Put it here where I can see it better. Oww! I've burnt myself. Here, take the plate back. Oooo!

Ho-ti   Put your fingers in your mouth, your Honour.

Judge   Mmmmm! Delicious! It melts in the mouth. I must have another taste. Pass that plate here. Mmmm! I have never tasted anything so wonderful.

Ho-wong   Your Honour, do you forget the case against our friend and neighbour, Ho-ti?

Judge   This is beautiful! Let me see . . . The case against Ho-ti. Mmm! Ho-ti, stand forth.

Ho-ti   Yes, your Honour.

Judge   Ho-ti, you are a man who knows much about pigs, are you not?

Ho-ti   I am, your Honour.

Judge   Then, Ho-ti, I would like you to buy me as many pigs as you can lay your hands on. I'll burn down my own house. Now, the case against Ho-ti and Bo-bo. Jurymen, have your made your decision?

Juryman II   We have, your Honour. Our verdict, after tasting the burnt pig, is 'Not Guilty'.

Judge   Then I pronounce Ho-ti and Bo-bo 'Not Guilty'.

Stage Manager   And so to the surprise of so many people Ho-ti and Bo-bo were released. It was not long before shrewd people noticed that the judge's house kept catching fire with pigs inside. Strangely enough, the same sort of thing seemed to happen fairly frequently with the jury members' houses. People all over the country began to discover the secret and soon houses were being burnt down every day. Of course, the cost of pigs and houses rose very sharply. Finally, someone discovered that it was not necessary to burn down a house in order to eat burnt pig and so pigs began to be cooked in more simple ways. And so we have the true story behind the origin of roast pig.

Questions

1 What did Ho-ti do when Bo-bo burned their house down?

2 Why did Ho-ti consider the loss of the pigs more important than the loss of the house?

3 Explain how Bo-bo came actually to taste roast pig?

4 What did Ho-ti do and say when he first tasted roast pig?

5 Why were Ho-ti and Bo-bo brought to trial?

6 Why was Ho-ti always happy when his house was burned down?

7 Why did the jury pronounce Ho-ti not guilty?

8 Why did the judge's house start catching fire?

9 Do you believe the Stage Manager when he says at the end of the play, 'And so we have the true story behind the origin of roast pig'? Why?

10 What part would you like to play in *The Origin of Roast Pig*? Why?

Red Hot Cinders

Richard Tydeman

Cast

Compere
Cinderella
Her Mother
Lily
Grace } Ugly Sisters
Fairy Godmother
Prince Charming
Herald
Mice, Rats, Courtiers, Guests at the Ball, etc.

ACT I

The **Compere** *appears before the curtain, carrying a full copy of the script to which he may — and should — refer from time to time.*

Compere   Kind friends, we now present before you,
      (And we hope we shall not bore you)
      A patent, potted Pantomime —
      Cinderella, all in rhyme.
      I'm the Compere or Commentator,
      And as you'll discover later
      I'm also prompter, hence my book;
      (Excuse me while I take a look)
      Ah, yes; now up the curtain goes.

    (**Compere** *moves to extreme L. of forestage. Curtain up, revealing* **Cinderella** *seated, in rags, weeping before the kitchen fire, L.*)

      And right before your very nose
      You see poor little Cinderella.

Cinders   I'm crying 'cos I've got no feller.

Compere   Well never mind, look not so glum
      Dear Cinderella, here's your Mum.

    (*Enter* **Mother** *R*).

Cinders   She's not my Mum, she's my step-mother;
      (We hate the sight of one another.)

Compere   The Mother speaks:

Mother   Now what's all this?
      Get up and help your sisters, miss!

Compere   And now here come the ugly sisters —
      A pair of most obnoxious blisters.

    (*Enter* **Ugly Sisters** *R.* **Lily** *is thin with a high voice;* **Grace** *is fat with a deep voice.*)

      What a figure! What a face!

Lily   My name is Lily.

Grace   Mine is Grace.

Lily   Now Cinders, do me up behind!

Grace   Come here now Cinders, never mind
About her buttons; do my hair!

*(**Cinderella** runs from one to the other.)*

Compere   So Cinders hurries here and there
Until they're ready to depart,
And Mum and ugly sisters start
To leave for good Prince Charming's Palace;

*(**Ugly Sisters** go off R. **Mother** gets to the exit.)*

But Cinderella, feeling 'jalous'
Says:

Cinders   Dear step-mother, can't I go?

Compere   But step-mamma just answers:

Mother   No! *(Exit **Mother**.)*

Compere   And now they're gone, poor Cinders cries
And holds her apron to her eyes;
But while she's wiping up her tears
Her Fairy Godmother appears.

*(Enter **Fairy Godmother,** and stand behind **Cinderella**.)*

Cinders   I *wish* that I could see the Ball!

Compere   The Fairy answers:

Fairy   So you shall!

Compere   Of course she should have said, 'You *shawl*',
         To rhyme with 'I could see the Ball'
         It's sometimes hard to make things rhyme,
         But then, who cares, in Pantomime?

Fairy   I am your Fairy God-mamma!

Cinders   Hurrah.

Compere   *(prompting)* Hurray.

Cinders   Hurray!

Compere   *(approving)* Hurrah.

Fairy   I wave my magic wand.

Compere   Hey presto!
         Rags are changed in evening dress to!

*(**Cinderella** throws off outer rags, disclosing Ball-dress.)*

Fairy   Fetch me a pumpkin, rat and mice.

Compere   And Cinders gets them in a trice.

*(Enter R., crawling, two **Mice** — small actors, one **Rat** — taller actor, covered with brown or grey blankets. **Cinderella** brings on a yellow balloon for a pumpkin.)*

Fairy   I wave my magic wand once more.

Compere   And up there rises from the floor
A Coach and Horses, all Complete
With Coachman. Cinders takes her seat.
But wait, the Fairy has not done:

Fairy   The Ball goes on till half past one;
But don't stay after twelve o'clock
Or else your shoes and lovely frock
Will change to rags. Now don't forget!

*(Exit all except **Compere**, L. — into fireplace, if any.)*

Compere   So off they go! And I will bet
That you all think it rather strange
They drive right through the kitchen range.
But I've seen stranger sights than these!
So ends Act One. The Curtains, please.

*(Curtains close, leaving **Compere** outside.)*

ACT II

Compere   There is no interval you know,
So we'll continue with the show.
The scene will look the same as ever,
But please imagine, if you're clever,
That we are at Prince Charming's house;
And hark! A dreamy waltz by Strauss.

*(The 'Blue Danube' is heard thumped out on a piano, or played on a very tinny gramophone. Curtain rises on several couples dancing. **Prince Charming** sits, C. Dance finishes, and dancers group L. and R.)*

See the happy dancers chaffing —
All except the Prince are laughing.
He's alone amidst the whirl:

Prince   I'm gloomy 'cos I've got no girl.

Compere   Well, cheer up Prince, two beauties come;
(It's Grace and Lily with their Mum.)

(Enter R. **Mother** *and* **Ugly Sisters***.)*

Mother   Your Royal Highness really oughter
Dance with this, my elder daughter.

(She pushes **Grace** *forward.* **Prince** *turns away.)*

Prince   Tonight no one shall dance with me;
I have a touch of Housemaid's Knee.

Compere   That isn't true. But do you blame him?
The ugly sisters, just to shame him,
Dance with each other.

(Ugly Sisters dance clumsily for a few bars.)

Oh, my hat.
We've had about enough of that!

(Enter Cinderella in Ball-dress, L.)

But who is this who now appears?
That guests all give three hearty cheers.
Hip hip . . .

Guests   Hurrah!

Compere   Hip hip . . .

Guests   Hurray!

Compere   Hip hip . . .

Guests   Hurrah!

Compere   I cannot say
What makes them happy. Yes I can —
They've seen the Prince — just watch that man,
He's positively truly bitten,
Not to say snookered, sunk, and smitten!

(Prince rises and meets Cinderella.)

Prince   Sweet lady, just one dance I crave.

Lily   Cheeky hussy!

Grace   Saucy knave!

Cinders   With you, dear Prince, I'd dance till dawn.

Lily   Well, chase me round the garden lawn!

(Prince and Cinderella dance for a few bars of soft music.)

1st Guest   I wonder who that girl can be?

Guests L.   We do not know.

Guests R.   And nor do we.

2nd Guest   Perhaps she is a Queen disguised?

Lily   She's overgrown!

Grace   She's undersized!

(Twelve bangs on a tin tray, off.)

Compere   The clock is striking twelve. Oh pray,
Cinderella, run away! *(Exit **Cinderella**, running.)*
But as she leaves, one shoe, size four,
Falls clattering on the Ballroom floor.
The Prince runs forward; picks it up;
He says:

Prince   I will not drink a cup
Of tea, nor eat my morning kipper,
Until I find who owns this slipper.

Compere   And now we'll leave this merry throng *(Curtain.)*
And draw the curtains. Not for long,
But just to indicate to you
That's the conclusion of Act Two.

ACT III

Compere   Now, for the last act of our play
We're back at Cinders' house, next day.

*(Curtain up. **Lily** discovered sitting, holding head; **Grace** standing, holding stomach.)*

What's this? The sisters — all alone?
Can it be hangovers they moan?

Lily   Oh my poor head!

Grace   Oh my poor tum!

Lily   I wish I hadn't had that rum.

Grace   I wish I hadn't had that jelly,
I've got a pain inside my . . .

Compere   Shelley!
Byron! Wordsworth! Keats! Defend us,
No words that rhyme with 'jelly' send us!

*(Enter **Mother,** R.)*

But here comes Mother with some news
That ought to chase away their blues.

Mother   The Prince's coach on the parade is.

Lily   Oh, tell the Prince to go to . . .

Compere   Ladies!

Mother   He's come to try the slipper, ducky;
Why shouldn't one of you be lucky?

Compere   The trumpet sounds. The cannons roar.

(*Appropriate noises from the wings.*)

The Prince is knocking at the door.

Herald   (*off*) Make way and let Prince Charming pass!

Compere   Then enter Prince, with slipper, glass.

(*Enter R.,* **Herald**, *carrying slipper on cushion,* **Prince Charming**, *and the* **Courtiers** — *formerly known as* **Guests**.)

Herald   All ladies who were at the Dance.
Can try this slipper.

Compere   What a chance
For these two girls.

Grace   (*sitting*) Now come on Lily,
Take my shoe off.

Lily   (*pushing* **Grace**) Don't be silly,
You're too old, and you're too fat.

Compere   Now ladies, not so much of that.
Toss up for first. Now you call, Grace.

(**Compere** *spins an imaginary coin.*)

Grace   I'll say it's heads.

Compere   It is. Now place
Your foot upon the Herald's cushion,
And see if the slipper you can push on.

(**Grace** *tries on the slipper.*)

Mother   Alas, your heel is much too large.

Grace   I'll grease it with a lump of marg.

Compere   Oh no, you won't. It's plain that you
Are not the owner of this shoe.

*(**Lily** takes **Grace's** place on the chair.)*

Mother   Let Lily try. Oh dear, your toe
Into the slipper will not go.

Lily   I'll cut it off and never wince.

Compere   No no! I'm very sorry, Prince,
At least, I mean I'm *glad* to state
You're saved from an unpleasant fate;
For neither margarine nor knife
Will fit these dames to be your wife.

*(Enter **Cinderella**, L., with rags on again.)*

Prince   Then let us go and try elsewhere.
But stay; who is this damsel fair?

Mother   Oh, just an orphan working here;
She was not at your Ball, I fear.

Compere   The Prince is not to be denied;

*(**Cinderella** sits and tries slipper.)*

He's tried for hours to find his bride.
And speaking between me and you,
I think he's getting hungry too,
For he has vowed he will not eat
Until he and his lady meet.

Herald   It fits. *(**Cinderella** throws off rags.)*

Lily   It can't!

Grace   Oh, what a cheek!

*(**Prince** and **Cinderella** embrace.)*

Compere   The Prince and Cinders cannot speak,
Except to say to Sis and Mother:

Prince
Cinderella } We're happy, 'cos we've got — each other.

Compere   They are too happy even to spy
That Fairy Godmamma is nigh.

*(Enter **Fairy Godmother**.)*

Come Fairy, Father Time is pressing;
Give the happy pair your blessing.

*(**Fairy Godmother** stands on chair.)*

Fairy   Bless you my children both, and may
All your troubles fly away.

(Tableau.)

Compere   Our play is done. My job is ended;
Now the least said, the soonest mended.
Music! Let curtains fall upon
The Wedding March by Mendelssohn.

(Piano or gramophone plays 'Wedding March'. Curtain falls — or better still, all characters march out in procession through the audience.)

THE END

Questions

1 Why is Cinders crying at the beginning of the play?

2 What is Cinders' attitude to her stepmother?

3 What is the compere's attitude to the ugly sisters?

4 How do the ugly sisters treat Cinders?

5 Why is the prince gloomy at the ball?

6 What is the prince's excuse for not dancing with the ugly sisters?

7 Why do the two ugly sisters dance together?

8 How does the prince react to Cinder's arrival at the ball?

9 How do the ugly sisters react to the arrival of the beautiful Cinders at the ball?

10 What scenery do you think would be needed for the staging of *Red Hot Cinders*?

Sitting on Top of the World

Allan Mackay

Introduction

The word 'comedy', when applied to a stage production, is a difficult word to define and it usually has to be preceded by a qualifying word such as 'Shakespearian' or 'Restoration' or 'black'. This play has no purpose other than to entertain through laughter. Its formula is a simple, imaginative set and the humour of the incongruous. Against a background of bizarre characters and near catastrophic events, Fred and Bill, the workmen, present an imperturbable, disinterested front. These two are the centre of the play. They should be acted in a laconic, unemotional way, even as disaster looms around them. Their actions should be minimal, even 'enforced'. This is not to say that their parts should be merely read. Vital to their characterization is their use of the dramatic pause to achieve the full comic effect, so their parts require quite a deal of skill to do them justice. To emphasize the incongruity of Fred and Bill's reactions, the other characters should be melodramatic, played with plenty of gusto.

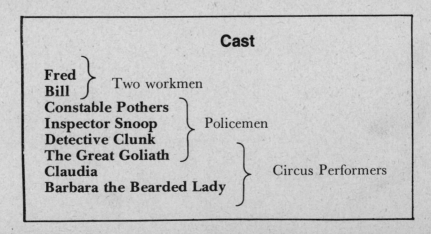

Cast

Fred
Bill } Two workmen

Constable Pothers
Inspector Snoop } Policemen
Detective Clunk

The Great Goliath
Claudia } Circus Performers
Barbara the Bearded Lady

SCENE

The stage represents the top of an uncompleted skyscraper, twenty-three storeys high. As work is in progress, various building materials lie about. At the back, piles of bricks are stacked, next to a cement mixer and bags of cement. Further down and slightly right is a wheelbarrow. Downstage right is a sawhorse, almost on the edge of the stage. The backdrop and side flats are painted to represent the sky, except to the left, where a small hut conceals an elevator shaft. This hut has a door in it, half facing the audience with the sign 'elevator' painted in crude letters on it.

It is the workmen's lunch hour. **Fred** *and* **Bill***, in overalls, are seated on the sawhorse,* **Bill** *to* **Fred's** *left. They are eating lunch from lunch-boxes held on their knees. About a yard farther left is a small flowerpot with a flower in it.*

Fred   Hey, Bill.

Bill   Yes, Fred?

Fred   It's a grand sight from up here.

Bill   *(looking straight out over the audience)* None better.

Fred   That's a fact, It's a grand sight.

   (There is silence. The men munch on their sandwiches.)

Fred   Bill, how much higher have we got to build this thing? We're twenty-three storeys up already.

Bill   Ask the boss when he gets back from lunch.

Fred   I don't think he knows, Bill.

Bill   Why do you say that, Fred?

Fred   I think he lost the plans. I asked him the other day and he got terrible upset.

Bill   Poor man.

   (Again silence. Then **Fred** *picks out a fresh sandwich and inspects its contents sadly.)*

Fred   Hey, Bill.

Bill   Yes, Fred?

Fred   Do you know my missus?

Bill Yes, Fred, I know your missus.

Fred Every day she packs sandwiches for my lunch. She said when we started this job that she'd pack me a different kind of sandwich for every storey we went up.

Bill Your missus is a very thoughtful woman. Fred.

Fred Oh, yes, she's thinking all the time.

*(Silence. **Bill** gets a fresh sandwich and starts eating.)*

Fred Bill, did you know there are twenty-three different ways of making egg sandwiches?

Bill Your missus is a very clever woman, Fred.

Fred That she is. But I'm getting terrible sick of egg sandwiches.

*(**Fred** suddenly throws the sandwich off the stage to his right. **Bill** takes no notice and continues eating. **Fred** takes out an apple and begins to polish it.)*

Bill Hey, Fred.

Fred Yes, Bill?

Bill Where did you throw that sandwich?

Fred Off the building, Bill.

*(**Bill** peers over the 'edge' of the building.)*

Bill You know, with the wind the way it is, it should land about the corner there.

*(**Fred** wets a finger and tests the wind.)*

Fred I reckon you're right, Bill.

Bill There's an old lady walking towards that corner.

Fred *(looking over)* It'll miss her by a yard. I didn't allow enough for the wind.

(He returns to his apple.)

Bill No, Fred, it'll hit her right on top of the head.

Fred Bill, do you want to make a bet on that?

Bill Yes, Fred. I'll bet you that apple against my banana it hits her.

Fred *(still not looking)* Your banana it is, Bill.

*(He continues to polish the apple. **Bill** looks over the edge. There is silence.)*

Bill Hey, Fred.

Fred Yes, Bill?

Bill You owe me an apple.

Fred *(handing over the apple)* You're a very clever man, Bill. Like my missus. *(He looks over and shouts)*, No, thank you, lady — I've finished with it.

*(Silence, **Bill** starts on the apple. **Fred** sadly nibbles at another sandwich.)*

Bill Yesterday I got a parson with my apple core.

Fred I didn't see you do that.

Bill Neither did the parson. He blamed the plasterers on the second floor.

Fred That must have been a good shot.

(Silence for a moment.)

Bill Fred, it wasn't such a good shot.

Fred Why's that, Bill?

Bill   I was aiming at the policeman directing traffic at the intersection.

Fred   Don't be too hard on yourself, Bill. The wind was tricky yesterday.

Bill   It was a bad day all round. I knocked a load of bricks off, too.

Fred   Bill, that was bad.

Bill   I'll say. The Boss said I had to pay for them. The missus was terrible upset. Do you know my missus, Fred?

Fred   Yes, Bill, I know your missus.

Bill   She was standing down there when I knocked the bricks off.

Fred   Yesterday certainly wasn't your lucky day, Bill.

Bill   I'll say. Every one of them missed her.

(Silence. They resume eating. **Bill** *looks sideways and sees the flowerpot).*

Bill   Hey, Fred.

Fred   Yes, Bill?

Bill   Where did you get the flower?

Fred   *(pointing)* That one, Bill?

Bill   It's the only one up here, Fred.

Fred   I got it on the fifth floor coming up this morning.

Bill   What was it doing down there?

Fred   I dunno. Growing, I suppose.

(A brief silence.)

Bill   Fred, why did you bring the flower up here?

Fred   Adds a touch of home.

Bill   I always said you were a man who loved nature, Fred.

(They return to their lunches. After a moment the elevator door opens and **Constable Pothers***, a young policeman, steps on the stage. He immediately begins to search among the bricks.* **Fred** *looks over his shoulder and sees him.)*

Fred   Hey, Bill.

Bill   Yes, Fred?

Fred A policeman just came up in the elevator.

Bill *(without looking)* Is that so? What's he doing?

Fred I dunno. Seems to be searching around.

Bill Perhaps he lost something.

(Silence. They eat for a while.)

Fred Bill, I don't think a policeman would lose anything 23 storeys up in the air.

Bill You're right, Fred.

Fred Bill, you haven't been caught lifting any of the company property, have you?

Bill Fred, that's a terrible thing to suspect of your working mate.

Fred Sorry, Bill.

(Silence for a moment.)

I should have known, you're too smart to get caught.

*(**Pothers** comes downstage to them. He looks very worried.)*

Pothers Pardon me.

(He gets no answer.)

Are you gentlemen workers on this building?

Bill No. I'm the Prime Minister and this is my wife. We come up here every lunch time for an egg sandwich and a cup of tea.

Pothers Oh, I see — you're pulling my leg.

Fred Bill, this young fellow is a terrible smart policeman.

Bill How do you work that out, Fred?

Fred He spotted straight away I wasn't your wife.

Bill You can't put anything over on the police, Fred.

Fred Yes, Bill. It makes you feel real safe.

Pothers *(in a dither)* It is my duty to ask that you leave this building. As a matter of fact, I must insist —

Fred Why? Are we out on strike?

Pothers   Good heavens, no. We had a telephone call that there's a bomb planted somewhere on one of the floors. It's timed to explode in twenty minutes!

*(There is no reaction from **Bill** or **Fred**.)*

Did you hear what I said? A bomb!

Bill   We heard, didn't we, Fred?

Fred   Yes, Bill. A bomb. Just like my car. Only it explodes every morning.

Pothers   *(very nervous)* Aren't you going? Aren't you even concerned?

Bill   Constable, this is our lunch hour and we don't have to shift from this seat until it ends. Union rules.

Pothers   But you have only twenty minutes. *(He looks at his watch.)* Nineteen.

Bill   Our lunch hour ends in twelve. We can be out of here in four. That gives us three left over. Am I right, Fred?

Fred   Yes, Bill, a ton of time.

Bill   Sit down, Constable, and have an egg sandwich.

Pothers   *(in dismay)* No, no — I couldn't!

Fred   Who wants to blow up this building? It isn't even finished.

Pothers   We don't really know. The telephone call came from an informer. Some madman must have slipped in early this morning and planted the bomb. We are fairly certain it is a new kind of explosive, very small and very powerful. Why, it could fit into almost anything, like that flowerpot there.

Fred Amazing what they can do these days, isn't it, Bill?

Bill That's a fact, Fred.

Pothers See here, you must go immediately. After all . . . I mean . . .

Bill Now, don't you worry about us. You'd better get your boys cracking and find that bomb, else our boss is going to be terrible upset.

Fred To say nothing of us, Bill.

Bill Why do you say that, Fred?

Fred I don't want to have to make a new start at ground level.

Bill No, Fred — that's an awful lot of egg sandwiches to go through again.

*(**Pothers** begins to back away, right.)*

Pothers I can't believe it. I tell you the building is going to explode and you just sit there and joke about it. I must report this to the Inspector . . .

(He backs off, right, still staring at the two men. They pay no attention and go on eating.)

Bill *(after a moment)* Hey, Fred.

Fred Yes, Bill?

Bill Can you still see that policeman?

*(**Fred** looks over the edge of the building.)*

Fred Yes. Bill. He's just passing the third floor now.

Bill Perhaps we should have told him the elevator was on the other side.

Fred I dunno. Bill. He looked like a young man who knew where he was going.

Bill *Was*, Fred?

Fred Yes, Bill. He's at the bottom now.

Bill Amen.

Fred Another two yards to the right and he'd have got that old lady cleaning egg sandwich off her head.

(They go back to eating. Then **Fred** *looks over.)*

Fred   Hey, Bill.

Bill   Yes, Fred?

Fred   Did you drop anything else over?

Bill   No, Fred. Why do you ask?

Fred   There's a big crowd gathering down there — and all looking up at us. That's a terrible temptation for a man who's still got five egg sandwiches in his lunch box.

Bill   They might be wondering who dropped a policeman.

Fred   Here comes the ambulance. Hey, there's a truck down there — looks like a circus truck.

(The elevator door opens and **The Great Goliath** *enters, accompanied by his wife,* **Claudia**. *They are both dressed in the colourful costumes of circus performers.* **Bill** *looks around and sees them.)*

Bill   Fred, it might have something to do with this fellow who has just come out on the roof.

Fred   *(still looking over)* What fellow's that, Bill?

Bill   Big chap with a funny costume on. Got his missus with him.

*(**Goliath**, his head held high, strides to centre stage. His wife follows, weighted down by a huge coil of rope.)*

Goliath   Where is the crowd?

Bill   *(pointing over)* Down there!

Goliath   The Great Goliath never looks down!

Bill   Neither do I when I'm dancing. You know my missus. Fred?

Fred   Yes, Bill. I know your missus.

Bill   She says I always pretend my feet aren't there when I'm dancing.

Fred   Your missus is a terrible quick mover, Bill.

Bill   She has to be, Fred.

Goliath   Today is a great moment in history. *(He strides around the roof.)* Today The Great Goliath will perform a feat never before equalled for its daring and danger.

Fred D'you think he's going to throw his missus off, Bill?

Goliath Today, Goliath will walk between this building and the one across the street — on this single strand of rope!

Bill Why don't you use the street. It's a whole sight bigger.

Goliath You do not understand. It has never been done before.

Bill I can believe that. This building wasn't here before.

(**Goliath** *comes up to him, threateningly.* **Bill** *ignores him.*)

Goliath Ha! You laugh at The Great Goliath and his death-defying rope-walking. Very well, he will show you! He will show the world! There is no one like Goliath! He is the best, the bravest —

Bill And the loudest.

Goliath Ha! Still you are not impressed. Then Goliath will do something that defies all human belief. He will carry his beloved wife across on one shoulder!

Bill I can believe that.

Fred Why do you say that, Bill?

Bill He's crazy.

Fred He must be, Bill — to risk his life like that.

Goliath You think Goliath is mad, do you? Goliath has carried his wife across Niagara Falls on a wire; he has carried her across the Grand Canyon; together they have looked down on the raging torrent of the Amazon from a rope of vines —

Fred   She must be a terrible brave woman, Bill.

Bill   That she must, Fred.

Claudia   No, no, you don't understand. We were only married yester-day and we're on our honeymoon. I'm Golly's fourth wife.

Bill   What happened to the first three?

Goliath   They . . . er . . . passed away early in life. They all suffered from a deadly disease, the falling sickness.

Fred   Aren't you afraid, Mrs. Goliath?

Claudia   Oh, no! I trust Golly. He's the first man I ever fell for — and the last.

(She looks lovingly at him.)

Bill   I can believe that.

Goliath   Are you ready, my dear?

Claudia   Yes, Golly.

Goliath   Then let us cast the rope. My assistant awaits on the other building to tie the end.

*(**Goliath** strides to the edge of the stage, right. The crowd can be heard, cheering. He stands erect, gazing ahead. Then he takes the rope from **Claudia** and prepares to throw it.)*

Fred   Hey, Bill.

Bill   Yes, Fred?

Fred   That's a terrible dangerous way to spend a honeymoon.

Bill   I dunno, Fred. I would say my honeymoon was more dangerous.

*(**Goliath** casts the rope. The crowd roars. **Claudia** claps excitedly.)*

Fred   Where did you spend your honeymoon, Bill?

Bill   With my mother-in-law.

Fred   Bill, you were lucky to come out alive.

*(**Goliath** has pulled the rope tight.)*

Goliath   Now we will tie this end to this wheelbarrow here. *(He does so.)* Good. We are almost ready.

*(He strides across and picks up the flowerpot. He speaks to **Fred** and **Bill**.)*

Especially for you, my friends, Goliath will add to the blood-chilling terror of his act. He will carry a flowerpot in his other hand.

(He returns to the edge of the roof.)

Are you prepared, my dear?

Claudia   Yes, Golly.

Bill   Any last requests?

Claudia   Oh, no.

Goliath   Up you go.

(He lifts her up on one shoulder. In the other hand he has the flowerpot.)

Claudia   Oooh, Golly, you are strong!

Goliath   Naturally. Wave to the crowd.

He steps off. Claudia waves and the crowd roars. The rope becomes tight.)

Fred   Hey, Bill.

Bill   Yes, Fred?

Fred   I hope he doesn't slip.

Bill   Why's that, Fred?

Fred   I was getting to like that flowerpot.

(Silence. They go back to their lunches. The wheelbarrow moves towards the edge of the stage.)

Bill   Where is he now, Fred?

*(**Fred** looks over his shoulder. The wheelbarrow moves another foot. The crowd roars.)*

Fred   Aboud halfway across.

(He turns back and takes another bite.)

Bill, I think you'd better go and sit in the wheelbarrow.

Bill   Why's that, Fred?

Fred   We'll lose it if you don't and you know how the boss feels about losing the tools.

Bill   Yes, Fred.

(He gets up and goes to the wheelbarrow, where he sits, looking out right.)

Fred   Is Goliath still there, Bill?

Bill   Yes, Fred. But he's going to have terrible trouble getting back.

Fred   Why's that, Bill?

Bill   Cause whichever way he goes, it's uphill.

(Suddenly he shouts.) Look out below!

Fred   Why did you say that, Bill?

Bill   Because he just dropped it.

Fred   A flowerpot can do an awful lot of damage, Bill. Just as well you warned them.

(Silence.)

Bill   Hey, Fred.

Fred   Yes, Bill?

Bill   It wasn't the flowerpot he dropped.

Fred   *(looking over)* Poor woman.

*(The elevator door opens and **Inspector Snoop** and **Detective Clunk** enter.)*

Snoop   Stop! Stop!

Fred   You'll have to shout louder. The lady can't hear you.

Bill   It's all right, Fred.

Fred   Why do you say that, Bill?

Bill   She's stopped.

Fred   Amen.

*(**Snoop** and **Clunk** come over to **Fred**.)*

Snoop   Where is The Great Goliath?

(**Fred** *points.* **Snoop** *goes to the edge of the stage, right.*)

Come back!

Goliath   *(off)* Goliath will never come back! He is going to jump and join his beloved!

Snoop   You can't do that! We need your help!

Goliath   *(off)* I must jump! Life has no meaning any more.

Snoop   Well, help us first, then jump afterwards.

Goliath   *(off)* That sounds like a good idea.

Clunk   Gentlemen, there is a bomb of tremendous power concealed on this building. It is timed to go off in ten minutes.

Bill   We know.

Clunk   You know? Then why are you still here?

Bill   Our lunch hour isn't up. *(He looks at his watch.)* Five more minutes yet.

Snoop   *(coming back)* It was planted by Barbara the Bearded Lady, a member of Goliath's Circus. She hates Goliath because he refuses to marry her.

Bill   *(looking over)* She's lucky.

Snoop   Anyway, she knew he was going to perform up here today and seized this chance to get rid of him while he was on the tightrope. We made investigations at the circus and Bobo the Clown told us.

Clunk   We've got to find that bomb!

*(The elevator opens and **Barbara the Bearded Lady** enters. She, too, is in costume and does indeed have a fine beard. She also has a gun which is pointed at the policemen.)*

Barbara   Stay where you are!

Snoop   It's Barbara!

Clunk   The Bearded Lady!

Barbara   You thought you could outwit me. Ha! Ha! But I followed you here from the circus. Ha! Ha! Now you are all going to die. Then no one will know who did this dreadful deed. Ha! Ha!

Bill   She's got a terrible strange sense of humour, Fred.

Fred   Reminds me of my missus, Bill.

Bill   She doesn't look a bit like your missus, Fred.

Fred   You're right, Bill. My missus has red hair.

Snoop   Bobo the Clown knows it was you.

Barbara   Ah, but tomorrow the circus will be looking for a new clown. Bobo has ceased to laugh — for ever. Ha! Ha!

Clunk   Barbara, innocent people will die.

Barbara   That cannot be helped. Ha! Ha! Where is Goliath?

Bill   Looking after his wife.

Barbara   Perfect! When the bomb explodes the rope will collapse and Goliath will take his last bow. But I must go. By the time the elevator returns it will be too late! Goodbye my friends — and happy landings. Ha! Ha!

(She goes out through the elevator. There is a stunned silence. No one moves.)

Fred   Hey, Bill.

Bill   Yes, Fred?

Fred   No more egg sandwiches.

Clunk   Inspector, we can't stand here and do nothing. We must find the bomb.

Snoop   Too late, too late.

Clunk   Well, we must get off the building.

Snoop   How? The only way down is the elevator.

Clunk   *(in dismay)* Then this is . . . it?

Snoop   I'm afraid so, Clunk. This is our last case.

Clunk   *(going to him)* Goodbye, Inspector. It's been a pleasure serving under you.

Snoop   Goodbye, Clunk. You've been a valiant friend . . . *(They shake hands sadly.)*

Bill   Hey, Fred.

Fred   Yes, Bill?

Bill   How fast would you say that elevator travels?

Fred   About eight miles an hour, Bill.

*(**Bill** does some mental calculations — counting on his fingers.)*

Bill   Then it should be passing the fourth floor by now, shouldn't it?

Fred   Right on the dot, Bill.

(**Bill** *wets a finger and holds it up to test the wind.*)

Bill   Wind's freshened.

Fred   That it has, Bill. Blowing from the south, I'd say.

(*More silent calculation. The policemen watch hopelessly.*)

Bill   Fred, how fast does a flowerpot fall?

Fred   Same speed as an egg sandwich, Bill.

(*More calculation.*)

Clunk   Thirty seconds, Inspector.

(**Bill** *suddenly shouts over the edge of the building.*)

Bill   Look out, below!

Snoop   What on earth are you doing?

Fred   Sssh — he's concentrating.

Bill   Mr. Goliath?

Goliath   (*off*) Yes?

Bill   Have you jumped yet?

Goliath   Not yet.

Bill   Good. Would you drop the flowerpot, please?

Fred   (*looking over*) Here comes Barbara.

Bill   And there goes the pot.

Fred   I think you'll miss, Bill.

Bill   (*no longer looking*) Not a chance.

(*There is the sound of an explosion below.* **Snoop** *and* **Clunk** *rush to the edge of the building, right.*)

Snoop   Good heavens, what was that?

Clunk   The bomb! It was in the flowerpot!

Snoop   Where's Barbara?

Bill   Just passing the eighth floor.

Snoop My dear fellow, you have saved our lives — and the building. I'll personally see that you get a medal for this fine deed. Come Clunk; we can finally fit the pieces of this case together.

(They hurry out through the elevator doors.)

Fred   Hey, Bill.

Bill   Yes, Fred?

Fred   Do you think we should have told them that the elevator is still on the ground floor?

Bill   No Fred. They'll find out when they get down there.

Fred   Our lunch hour is up.

Bill   So it is, Fred. Back to work.

(He gets up and comes forward. The wheelbarrow disappears over the edge of the building.)

Fred   Bill, we just lost the wheelbarrow. It's gone.

*(**Bill** goes to the edge, right.)*

Bill   So has Goliath. What a dreadful thing to happen.

Fred   Yes, Bill. The boss is going to make us pay for that wheelbarrow.

*(**Fred** gets up and goes to the pile of bricks at the back.)*

Bill   At least they're together.

Fred   Who's that, Bill?

Bill   Goliath and Barbara.

Fred   I always said you were a romantic man, Bill.

Bill   That I am, Fred. I like to see love stories end up right.

(**Fred** *brings the pile of bricks up front and stacks them near the sawhorse.*)

Bill   Hey, Fred.

Fred   Yes, Bill?

Bill   That Barbara didn't look anything like your missus.

Fred   Why do you say that, Bill?

Bill   Your missus hasn't got a beard.

(**Fred** *lays the bricks out in a line across the stage. Then he stops.*)

Fred   Hey, Bill.

Bill   Yes, Fred?

Fred   I just worked something out.

Bill   What's that, Fred?

Fred   You don't know my missus.

BLACKOUT — CURTAIN

Questions

1   Why does Bill feel the previous day was a 'bad day all round'?

2   Explain why Bill and Fred refuse to move immediately when Constable Pothers tells them about the bomb.

3   Why is the big crowd down below a 'terrible temptation' for Fred?

4   When Goliath says his earlier wives died of 'the falling sickness' we, the audience, can see a second meaning behind his words. What is the second meaning that we see?

5   Explain the double meaning behind Claudia's words as she speaks of Goliath: 'He's the first man I ever fell for — and the last'.

6   Find two other examples of lines with double meanings from the play.

7   Why does tying his rope to the wheelbarrow turn out to be a mistake by Goliath?

8   Why does Bill ask Goliath to drop the flowerpot at the particular moment he does?

9   How would you describe, for someone who didn't know them, what Bill and Fred are like? Write two sentences describing the character of each.

10   At the end, how does Fred work out that Bill really doesn't know his missus?

Werewolf in Town

Lewis Gardner

PART ONE
A BOY LEAVES HOME

Narrator   Oak Valley was like 10,000 other towns — except for one difference. In a neat little house on Elm Street, there lived a boy with a problem.

Tommy   *(howling like a wolf)* Oww-woooooooo!

Narrator   It happened every month when the full moon rose in the sky. Long hairs came out on his forehead and his hands. Two of his teeth grew into long, sharp fangs. And he couldn't stop howling at the moon.

Tommy   Oww-woooooooo!

Narrator   Yes. Tommy was a werewolf.

Tommy   Why does it have to happen to me? Other kids don't worry about the moon. They can go right on doing their homework or watching television. Not me. Oww-woooooooo!

Narrator   All over town, the citizens wondered what the sound was.

Citizen 1   What is that?

Citizen 2   Is it a wild dog?

Citizen 3   Is it a wolf?

Citizen 4   It must be the teenagers, fooling around.

Narrator   Every month, Tommy became very worried.

Tommy   What if my parents find out?

*(He joins his **parents** and **sister** at the breakfast table.)*

Father   You're late for breakfast, Thomas.

Tommy   Sorry.

Father   You shouldn't sleep so late. It's bad for your character.

Mother   You look tired, Tommy. Did you sleep well?

Sister   *I* didn't. All night long, I heard that sound. Some kind of dog — or a wolf.

Mother   I heard it too, dear. It was probably an owl.

Sister   It was a wolf.

Father   There haven't been wolves in this part of the country for 100 years.

Sister   Then it's a *werewolf.*

Tommy   *(choking on his food)* Awrk!

Father   Chew your food carefully, Thomas, and you won't choke.

Mother   A what, dear?

Sister   A werewolf. A man who becomes a wolf when the moon is full.

Mother   That's nonsense. You've been reading too much.

Father   You should get more exercise. It's better for your character. *(**Tommy** gets up.)* Where do you think you're going, young man?

Tommy   Back to bed. I feel too sick to go to school today.

Father   He'll turn into a bum some day. No character.

Narrator   As a child, Tommy had seemed like a normal little boy.

Tommy   *(as a little boy)* I don't like this story, Mommy.

Mother   Why don't you like it, Tommy?

Tommy   Little Red Riding Hood gets off free at the end. But they shoot the poor old wolf. That isn't fair!

Mother   But the wolf was *bad*, Tommy. He wanted to *kill* the little girl.

Tommy   *(with a wild smile)* Yeah! *(He turns to his **father**.)* Daddy, why does the wolf always have to lose? He even lost to those three slobby little pigs!

Father   The purpose of these stories is to develop character, Thomas. You're supposed to *like* the three little pigs.

Narrator   Later, as an unhappy teenager, Tommy tried to get help. One day, he read an advice column in a newspaper. Tommy decided to write.

Tommy   *(writing)* 'Dear Clarissa Velveteen, I have a problem.' *(He crumples up the paper.)* What's the use? How could she tell me what to do?

Narrator   Tommy went to see the guidance counsellor at school.

Guidance Counsellor   Sit down, Tommy. What's bothering you?

Tommy   I'm a werewolf.

Guidance Counsellor   Well, perhaps you'd enjoy a career as a night watchman in a factory.

Tommy   I wasn't making plans for the future. I'm a werewolf *now*.

Guidance Counsellor   Well, I think you should make more friends in school. Take part in extra-curricular activities. Or find a part-time job.

Tommy   *(without hope)* Thank you.

Narrator   Next, Tommy saw the family doctor.

Tommy   Doc, you've taken care of me since I was a baby.

Doctor   Have I?

Tommy   I was much smaller then.

Doctor   I think I remember.

Tommy   Well, I have a problem. I'm a werewolf.

Doctor   Have you been getting plenty of fresh air and exercise?

Tommy   Yes, I run through the woods and the hills. I howl at the moon.

Doctor   Here are some pills to calm you down. They'll make you forget you're a werewolf.

Tommy   *(without hope)* Thank you.

Narrator   Tommy decided to tell his father.

Tommy   Dad, are you busy?

Father   I'm trying to do something with the bills. In one pile I put the bills we won't pay this month. The other pile is for the bills we won't pay next month, either.

Tommy   Dad, I have a problem.

Father   I don't know how your mother spends so much on food every month.

Mother   Sometimes I think someone is eating raw meat out of the refrigerator. It disappears about once every month.

Tommy   That's exactly what I —

Father   My dear wife, what kind of stupid remark is that? You sound more like your mother every day.

Mother   Let's leave my mother out of this. Now *your* mother —

Tommy   Mom, Dad, I —

Father   My mother —

Narrator   Tommy decided it wasn't the right time to tell his parents.

Tommy   *He* would say, "Sure, he takes after your side of the family.' *She* would say, 'He's just like his father. He's just more open about it.'

Narrator   For a werewolf in a small town, life can be lonely. Tommy was afraid to hang around with the other teenagers, especially at night. Bull Hawkins, the leader of the Evil Angels gang, liked to pick on him.

Bull   What's the matter with you, Tommy? We never see you at the hamburger joint, making faces at the cops like a normal guy. Won't your mother let you out at night? *(Shoves **Tommy**.)*

All the Evil Angels   Get him, Bull! Get him! Break him in two! *(They all laugh.)*

Narrator   But joy will sweeten even the most unhappy life. After lunch at school, Tommy used to lean against his locker, while everyone else talked or played cards. One day, he noticed a girl who was leaning against *her* locker.

Tommy   *(shyly)* Hi.

Lily   Hi, I'm Lily. I'm new here. I'm glad to meet you.

Tommy   Hi.

Lily   If you want to know me better, why don't you take me out Saturday night?

Tommy   Saturday?

Lily   What's wrong? Don't you like me?

Tommy   How about next Tuesday?

Lily   Saturday or never. There's a full moon that night.

Tommy   I know.

Lily   We can take a walk in the moonlight.

Tommy   Look, there's something you should know about me. I'm not like the other kids around here.

Lily   I know. You're kind, and you're sweet.

Tommy   There's something a little *funny* about me. You'll find out, and you'll hate me.

Lily   Don't you think I can like you enough so I won't *care* if there's something funny about you? Please believe me.

Tommy   Yes! I believe you!

Lily   I'll see you Saturday at 8.00. We can meet at the edge of the woods.

Narrator   For the next few days, Tommy was walking on air.

Tommy   Maybe the calendar is wrong. Maybe the moon won't be really full until Sunday night.

Narrator   However, you can guess what happened.

Lily   Where *is* that sweet boy? It's two minutes after 8.00. Is he standing me up? Oh, that must be —

Tommy   Lily! Lily! Oww-woooooooo! Oww-woooooooo!

Lily   *(screaming):* Ahhhh!

Narrator   Lily ran away.

Lily   Help! Help! A werewolf!

Tommy   And she said she wouldn't care if there was something funny about me.

Narrator   Tommy hid in the woods, howling every few minutes. Lily stirred up the town.

Lily   A werewolf! A werewolf!

All the Citizens   A werewolf!

Tommy   Oww-woooooooo!

Citizen 1   We've got to catch him!

Citizen 2   We can't let someone go around scaring our kids.

Lily   *(crying)* He ate Tommy!

Citizen 3   He must be caught!

All the Citizens   He ate Tommy!

Mother   Poor Tommy!

Father   I knew this would happen.

Tommy   *(hearing them as they come closer)* At least they don't know I'm Tommy! *(Sirens are heard)* Oww-woooooooo! There I go again.

Citizen 4   There he is!

Citizen 1   After him!

Narrator   Bull Hawkins and the Evil Angels were looking for some fun. They joined the Chief of Police and his men in the search.

Bull   Who's afraid of a werewolf anyway?

Narrator   After 10 minutes in the woods, there were three strange howls.

Tommy   Oww-woooooooo!

Bull   *(in pain)* Eee-Yowww!

Evil Angels   Yowww!

Narrator   Bull Hawkins and the Evil Angels came running out of the woods.

Evil Angels   Help! The werewolf! Help!

Bull   He bit me! He bit me! And he ripped my leather jacket!

Narrator   The search went on until the moon went down. The sky was becoming light with the approach of daybreak. Tommy snuck out of the woods — and met the Chief of Police!

Chief of Police   Who's there?

Tommy   Please! Listen! I can explain!

Chief   Don't worry, Tommy. It's all right now. A werewolf doesn't come after you every day.

Narrator   Tommy felt his forehead and teeth. He realized he was back to normal.

Tommy   No, I guess he doesn't.

Chief   So run on home now. Your parents will be glad to see you.

Narrator   Tommy started walking home.

Tommy   I can't face them again. People will remember things I've said. And the moon will be full again. There's nowhere I can hide!

Narrator   Tommy made a decision.

Tommy   I'm leaving home!

Narrator   So Tommy took a bus to another state. He found a commune in the mountains where the people were happy to take him in — even when he told them about his condition.

Commune Member   So what? I get ingrown toenails every now and then.

Narrator   Tommy helped with the farming and the other work of the commune. For the first time since his childhood, Tommy felt hopeful about life.

PART TWO
TOMMY FINDS A HOME

Narrator   Life on the commune was happy until an accident happened.

Commune Member   Look, man, you know you're welcome to stay here. You're a good worker, and we think your howling is groovy. But we can't afford to lose any more chickens. So be careful next month. Okay man?

Tommy   Okay.

Narrator   Tommy decided to help out by getting a part-time job.

Tommy   I want to pay for some new chickens.

Narrator   He went to work in a diner in a nearby town. It was called Joe's Cafe.

Joe   Say, Tommy, you're a good worker. You have a way with a scrambled egg. How about working the night shift? You'll get better tips.

Tommy   No, Joe. No, I really can't.

Joe   What a bunch I've got working for me! Mary won't work nights, either.

Mary   I've told you before, Joe. I just can't.

Narrator   Mary Wolf was the lovely girl who worked behind the counter with Tommy.

Tommy   She has such nice, kind eyes. And I'd like to stroke her smooth, dark hair.

Narrator   One day, it was the end of their workday.

Mary   It's 6.00. Time for us to hang up our aprons and go home.

Tommy   Yes.

Mary   Full moon tonight.

Tommy   I know.

Mary   Where's Joe? I want to get home as soon as I can.

Tommy   Me, too.

Mary   Do you still live on the commune?

Tommy   Oh, yes.

Mary   I'd like to see it sometime.

Tommy   Oh, yes.

Mary   What's the matter with you? Can't you talk?

Tommy   Oh, Mary, I love —

  (The telephone rings.)

Joe   *(on telephone)* Mary, this is Joe. My car is stuck. You and Tommy will have to keep the place open until I can get there.

Mary   Joe, I've told you I can't work at night.

Joe   As a favour to me?

Mary   Okay.

Narrator   As it grew darker outside, Tommy became more and more worried. He turned away from the customers as much as he could. He kept looking in the shiny part of the coffee machine to see if there were any signs of a change. He could see Mary acting funny, too.

Tommy   I must be making her nervous.

Narrator   Finally, he couldn't stand it any more. He looked out the window. He saw the first rays of the full moon! Tommy started running out the front door. Mary was running out too. She pushed by him. Joe was coming in right then.

Joe   Thanks, kids. *(He steps out of the way.)* They sure are in a hurry.

Narrator   Tommy could feel the fur on his face. He saw it on his hands. He ran into the woods.

Tommy   I have to get away, before I do my first howl. Where's that hill I saw last month? Over there!

Narrator   As he ran up the hill, he heard a sound that was strange, yet familiar.

Mary   *(howling like a wolf)* Oww-woooooooo!

Tommy   Mary!

Mary   Tommy!

Tommy   Mary!

Mary   Tommy!

Mary and Tommy   Oww-woooooooo! Oww-woooooooo! *(The howling fades away.)*

Narrator   Tommy and Mary are happy today. They have their own little house on the commune. The other members lock up the chickens on certain nights. And everyone likes their charming little baby. Tommy is teaching him how to hunt, so the commune will have food and warm clothes. Mary is teaching him how to sing to the moon.

Mary   *(reading)* 'So the wolf swallowed Little Red Riding Hood, and he lived happily ever after.'

Questions

1   Though the Narrator says Tommy was a normal little boy, what is there about his reaction to some bedtime stories that seems a little different?

2   What happens when Tommy tries to tell his parents about his problem? Why does he decide not to tell them?

3   Why does Tommy risk meeting Lily, even though he knows the moon will be full that night?

4   How does Tommy get revenge on Bull Hawkins and The Evil Angels?

5   What does the Chief of Police conclude when he finds Tommy returning from the woods?

6   What finally makes Tommy decide to leave home?

7   Explain why Tommy is happier living at the commune in the hills.

8   Why is Mary unwilling to work nights at the diner?

9   How does Mary change the ending of *Little Red Riding Hood* when she reads it to their son at the end of the play?

10   Explain the writer's reason for using a Narrator as one of the characters in the play. What purpose is served by having a Narrator?

Nutty News

Clifford Powell

Introduction

In a number of television comedy shows of recent years a humorous newscast has been done. Perhaps the best known of these is that done by Ronnie Barker and Ronnie Corbett in *The Two Ronnies*. The following script is their kind of 'news'. One way of using the script, and involving every class member at some point, is to set up the desks in a circle around the classroom. A portable 'mike' can be used by the person reading, and this can be passed on to the next person as the next snippet is read. Alternatively, a news team of five (or two!) could be given the task of preparing and presenting the whole news.

Each snippet is given a new number, but it is up to you to settle on how your class will use the material!

Good Evening.

1 Good evening, ladies and gentlemen, nice to be with you again.

2 And in a packed show tonight, we'll be telling you about a male and a female astronaut who met each other while orbiting the earth. Reports indicate they are still going around together.

3 And we give you the inside information on how to drive a baby buggy — tickle its feet!

4 And we reveal the truth about the age of evergreen filmstar Ed Urkie. He claims to be a young colt, but actually he's an old forty-five.

5 And we'll be looking into the case of Angus McCompton, the Scotsman who always treated his own illnesses by consulting medical textbooks.

6 He died recently of a typographical error! We'll also be asking the searching question 'Should every visitor to Central Railway Station wear platform soles?'

7 And we run an in-depth interview with Cecil Swindle, the world's greatest liar. When he says 'Good morning!' people ring the weather bureau to check up!

8 And we carry on interviewing with Eustace Filp who, at the age of eight, ran away with Sole Bros. Circus. He has, at last, brought it back.

9 And we were to have brought you an interview with the world's dumbest man, but, unfortunately, he lost his mind yesterday when kicked in the head by a butterfly.

10 Every time he gets into a taxi the driver keeps the 'Vacant' sign up.

11 But later on tonight we'll be discussing the problems of Red China — does it look best on a white table-cloth or not?

12 And we'll be reporting an interview with the overwhelmed tourist who stood by the banks of the Grand Canal in Venice, just drinking it all in . . .

13 While his wife stood alongside the gorgeous display windows of a nearby shop, just reflecting . . .

14 And we'll be offering some advice to fathers whose sons have just acquired their licences and want to borrow the family car —

15   Don't stand in their way.

16   And we'll be thinking of those of you who are wondering if you should get your eyes checked. Why not stick to the colour you've got now.

17   But first the news . . .

18   Reports at hand indicate that Toby Arbuckle, well-known TV celebrity arrived at the studio drunk yesterday and was instantly dismissed. The Channel manager has issued a press release which says, 'He was loaded, so I felt he should be fired.'

19   While on the island of Okinawa yesterday, three Japanese seamen, stranded after their fishing boat sank, were fired upon by trigger-happy U.S. Occupation troops.

20   The Japanese retaliated by throwing transistor radios, cameras and tape recorders, but were overpowered.

21   World opinion about the incident has varied from brief comments in Tokyo newspapers to headlines in the New York Times 'Yanks Win War in Pacific'.

22 Dr Christian Barnard, South Africa's famous surgeon, has just performed the world's first navel transplant — on a belly dancer from Istanbul.

23 Unfortunately, the patient died. The matter has now been declared a major Turkish navel disaster.

24 While, in Bavaria today, the wife of a German shepherd gave birth to eleven offspring.

25 Both mother and pups are doing well.

26 And we break in to report that following an argument, Brazilian golfer, Roberto de Fisto has shot his partner, Juan. He later boasted to police, 'I made a hole in Juan'.

27 Mr Axel Ryber of Matraville, who has two wooden legs, had his home catch fire yesterday. It seems they managed to save the house but Mr Ryber was burnt to the ground.

28 And, in a report from the Fire Insurance Company, it appears that Mr Ryber will not receive any insurance. The company claims Mr Ryber hasn't a leg to stand on.

29 And, in a burglary last night at the home of Sydney University's Professor Pendlebury, thieves stole two of the professor's most valuable books. 'The thing that upsets me most,' reported the Professor, 'is that I hadn't finished colouring one of them in.'

30 While, at Melbourne's Central Court today, a boy was charged with breaking every window in his house with an axe. The judge acquitted the boy because he came from a broken home.

31 This is the same judge who recently dismissed the case against a woman charged with murdering her husband, on the grounds that she was a widow and had no visible means of support.

32 And, from Canberra, we report that Australia's Minister for Pollution, Sir Willy Smellieperson, has changed his name by deed poll. In future he will be known as Sir Charlie Smellieperson.

33 While, from overseas, it has been reported that Britain's Prime Minister has criticized the way Britain is always reported to be 'expecting' something. He cited examples such as 'Britain expecting to control inflation shortly', 'Britain expecting to bring down unemployment' and 'Britain expecting to obtain a favourable balance

of trade'. He said that in the eyes of the world Britain was always expecting something. He felt that this was largely responsible for Britain being known as the Mother Country.

34 And, in Scotland, the Glasgow Health Department has scotched rumours of an outbreak of bubonic plague. Fears were aroused initially when four Scotsmen were admitted to hospital with black tongues. However, it was later discovered that the men had dropped a bottle of whiskey on a freshly-tarred road.

35 While, on the industrial scene in Sydney, waterside workers have gone on strike again.

36 This time they want fairy bread for morning tea.

37 And, in Brisbane, police have found abandoned a semi-trailer, hijacked overnight with its load of licorice all-sorts. All the contents are reported to have gone. In a special announcement the head of Brisbane C.I.B. said today, 'We believe the thieves are still on the run'.

38 And, on the sporting scene, we report an incredible return to form by West Australian batsman, Phil Tonka. Apparently Phil ate a packet of prunes before going in to bat in the match against Queensland, and made a hundred runs before lunch.

39 And the New South Wales Salesmen's Conference has just announced its winner for the Salesman of the Year Award. The coveted prize goes to George Filbert for his effort in selling two milking machines to a farmer with only one cow — and taking the cow as a down payment.

40 Results of the Sydney Football Pools are to be announced next week. Sydney folk are reminded of the prizes — First prize, one week's holiday in Melbourne; Second prize, two weeks' holiday in Melbourne . . .

41 And, overseas, authorities at the Kruger National Park in South Africa have admitted that they have been unable to stem the widespread slaughter of the gnu (spelt g-n-u)! Hunters have recently engaged in such slaughter that the species is now extinct.

42 And so that brings us to the end of the gnus.

For you to try

Now that you've had a try at a class news-reading, set to work writing your own. All it needs is for each member of the class to produce one or two humorous news items of the kind used by the two Ronnies, and then for someone (or a small team) to put it all together, and edit the final versions. Borrow a joke-book from the library if you need inspiration, or try re-working one of your favourite gags into the form of a news item. Once you get the hang of it you'll find it isn't too difficult — and it's a tremendous amount of fun. Away you go!

Boots An' All

Allan Mackay

Cast

The Coach
The Team
    Forwards   Brewster (Captain)
                               Murphy
                               Phillips
                               Winston
                               Carew
                               Bailey
    Backs   Soliman
                                 Shaw
                               Allen
                               Tulley
                               Waite
                               Grant
                               Tremain
    Reserves   Brooks
                               Rankin
The School Reporter   Gribble

SCENE

The dressing room adjacent to a football oval. To the right and left, and set obliquely on the stage, are two low benches facing inward to the centre. Behind these, and running across the stage, is a row of metal lockers, most hanging open and adorned with pieces of clothing. These lockers may be painted on a backdrop. Small carry bags, shoes, towels, etc. are scattered around. There is only one door and that is to the right.

*At the moment the room is being used by a school football team, just prior to a game. The **Coach**, a very young, bespectacled man in ill-fitting track suit, is standing down centre, facing the audience. He is energetically performing warm-up exercises. Behind him are the thirteen members of his team and two **Reserves**. The **Forwards** are roughly grouped in front of the right bench, the **Backs** in front of the left. The **Reserves** are standing behind them and off to the left. To the right stands **Gribble**, the school reporter, wearing a huge sign on his lapel which says 'Press' and carrying an enormous first aid case. He is smirking with enjoyment and as the play begins, he puts down the case and starts taking notes in a small book. The team looks anything like a football team. Their uniforms are outsize and undersize and their whole attitude suggests a profound desire to be anywhere but here. Apparently, they are supposed to be following their **Coach** in the exercises but their dedication doesn't extend that far. Most are slumped on the benches, a few stand sloppily, half-heartedly doing a few abbreviated exercises.*

Coach   Right, boys — just a few more warm-up exercises before we get out there! Now, all together — with me — one, two — one, two — one, two — *(He continues to perform the exercises with much enthusiasm — and absolutely no response from his charges. Then he stops, takes a deep breath, and turns around. Just before he does so, however, the boys, rising to the occasion, spring to attention and manage to appear, at least to the **Coach's** devoted eyes, like a team that has just undergone extreme physical exertion. Much heavy breathing, mopping of brows, etc. As he speaks, they slump as one on the benches, the **Forwards** on the right, the **Backs** on the left, the **Reserves** still standing — **Gribble** still smirking and starting to take notes.)*

Coach   Ah, that's better. Nothing like a few knee-bends to tone up the muscles, eh?

(The boys mumble grimly in agreement.)

Didn't tax you too much, did I?

(Much shaking of heads.)

Don't want to take the shine off you, do I?

(More shaking of heads, less enthusiastically.)

You getting this all down, Gribble?

Gribble   Oh, yes sir — every last physical jerk.

Coach   Good. *(He strides upstage and turns so that he is between the two benches.)* Right, boys — ten minutes till kick-off! Ten minutes till we come face to face with Saxby High!

(A look of horror flashes on the faces of the boys. Indeed several seem close to fainting.)

And this — *this* is the big one! Boys — I want to feel like I'm having trouble holding you back. Like you're dead keen to jump out there and give them all sorts of hell. That's what I want to feel. Show me that's how I should feel, boys!

(But the boys by this time are looking decidedly distressed. Still the **Coach** *is undaunted.)*

Now, listen carefully. Gribble over there has been in the Saxby High dressing room and he swears they're scared stiff.

*(**Gribble** starts to protest but is interrupted.)*

Scared stiff, I tell you! Now — what are they scared of?

Brewster   Getting arrested for murder, sir?

Coach   Veeeery funny, Brewster. Always got the last minute joke, haven't you! Boys, they're scared of us! Imagine that!

Brewster   I can't, sir. Can any of you fellas imagine it?

(Much shaking of heads.)

Gribble   They weren't actually scared, sir. They were more . . . well . . . .

Coach   *(prompting)* Nervous?

Gribble   No, sir — laughing. Geez, you guys, ya shoulda heard 'em laugh. I thought their coach was gunna split a gut —

(All of which has a tremendous effect on the team.)

Coach   Shut up, Gribble! Boys, they're afraid of what we're going to do to them. And what are we going to do to them?

Brewster You'd better tell us, sir, so we'll know.

Murphy Yeah, an' then flash over an' tell Saxby so's they'll know, too.

Coach We're going to smash 'em, grind 'em into the ground, hit 'em boots an' all! We're going to plough right into 'em an' pound 'em so hard, they'll wish they'd never heard of us!

*(Unfortunately the **Coach** is the only one convinced.)*

Brewster I don't think they *have* heard of us, sir.

Coach We're going to tear into 'em with all we've got! We're going to pick 'em up and spear 'em into the ground so hard they'll think —

*(But this is too much for **Bailey**.)*

Bailey Ooooh, stop it, sir — I feel sick in the stomach.

Coach *(carried away)* They'll be the sick ones, won't they boys? *(A determined silence. The **Coach** repeats himself fiercely.)* Won't they?

Team *(very unconvinced)* Yes, sir. I suppose so, sir, etc.

Coach That's better. *Now* we're on the right track. It doesn't matter that they're leading the comp. and we're coming eighth —

Murphy Which is last.

Coach Eighth! Remember that, Murphy — only seven from the top! It doesn't matter that they haven't lost a game and we haven't won one, does it?

Phillips It does worry us a little, sir.

Coach And so it should but now you can forget it, because we've been saving ourselves for the big one!

Bailey The big what, sir?

Phillips He must mean their big lock. You'll be markin' him, Bailey. Have ya seen him?

Bailey *(quailing)* N-N-No. . .

Winston I have. Built like a train, only faster.

Phillips I reckon they oughta give him a blood test to see if he's human.

Bailey   Oh, gawd!

Coach   Quiet! I meant the big game — the one we've been waiting for.

Phillips   Yeah — like waitin' in the middle of the track for the express to come through. Wham! Squirt! An' you're one inch thick all over the rails!

Coach   That's nonsense, Phillips.

Phillips   Yeah — well how come no one's scored a point against Saxby yet, sir?

Coach   Luck of the draw. Saxby hasn't played *us* yet!

Gribble   I think that's why they were laughing, sir.

Coach   Now come on, boys, don't believe every wild story you hear.

(But now the rot has set in.)

Brewster   They beat Marsden High fifty to nil!

Murphy   Yeah — an' the game was called off at half time.

Phillips   Why?

Murphy   Marsden wouldn't come back on the field.

Winston   A kid from Marsden told me none of his team could walk.

Carew   Eight of 'em had broken legs an' they were the lucky ones!

Murphy   Yeah — and Marsden beat *us* forty to nil.

Bailey   Oh, gawd!

*(Now the **Backs** join in the general panic.)*

Soliman   Saxby beat Green Hills High sixty to nil!

Shaw   Five kids were taken to hospital!

Allen   In ambulances — one for each kid! You could hear the sirens all over town!

Shaw   They ain't out yet an' the game was a month ago.

Allen   One of 'em is but he's still on crutches.

Tulley   They reckon the hospital called for blood donors. Fifty turned up but it wasn't enough —

(Waving arms frantically, the **Coach** *tries to stop the retreat.)*

Coach   Boys, boys, boys! You're starting to panic! You're beaten before you go on —

Brewster   Then we might as well call the game off, sir. Right you guys — back to school —

(There is a mass movement for the door.)

Coach   Stay where you are!

(Reluctantly they sink back on the benches.)

I won't listen to all this coward's talk! We're going to win this one and win well, if it's the last thing we do!

Brewster   It pro'bly will be.

Coach   We've trained specially for it and we're ready!

Brewster   Ready to get crunched.

Coach   Stop it, Brewster! As the captain, I expect better of you. You should set an example, lead your men —

Brewster   That just means I'll be the *first* to get crunched.

Coach   Rot! If anyone's going to get crunched, it'll be Saxby — boots an' all!

Bailey   I wish you'd stop talkin' about boots, sir.

(At this, a new panic hits the ranks like an ocean wave.)

Murphy   Saxby boys've got iron studs on their boots.

Phillips   Yeah — an' they use 'em to rake right up from ya mouth to ya eyeballs. First, out comes ya front teeth — craaaack! Then ya nose gets worked over — wooosh! An' ya face is like a peeled tomato — splat!

Bailey   Oh, gawd. . .

Phillips   Yeah — an' they stomp on ya throat while yer gettin' up — gawk! Out comes ya tongue and blam! — down comes the other boot on it — squelch!

Murphy   This Marsden kid got booted in the gut in a scrum. He was lyin' on the ground screamin' an' the whole Saxby team ran up an' jumped on his head.

Phillips   Crrrr-ump!

Coach   Stop it, stop it — all of you! I've never heard such disgraceful talk! It's just a pack of lies! Fairy tales! Do I make myself clear?

Team   *(barely audible)* Yes . . . sir.

Coach   I want you to get out there and show them what you're made of —

Phillips   They'll see soon enough — blood an' bones an' mush.

Coach   The headmaster and the whole school will be watching. Let's make them proud of us.

Brewster   It's hard to make people proud when ya gettin' crunched, sir.

Coach   For the last time . . . *(He suddenly notices **Gribble** taking notes.)* Gribble, you're not writing all this down, are you?

Gribble   You said to, sir. Pre-match report for the school newspaper.

Coach   I didn't mean *everything*. Just the . . . good bits.

Gribble   But I've *got* to write something, sir.

Coach   Why, lad?

Gribble   'Cause I don't think there'll be much to write about *after* the match. *(He grins.)* This paper don't print obituaries.

Coach   Very smart. Give me that pad.

Gribble   It's only notes, sir.

Coach   Give it here!

*(Reluctantly **Gribble** comes across and hands over the pad. The **Coach** looks at it. His eyes widen in shock.)*

Gribble, you little worm — you're running a book on the game. You're . . . taking bets!

Soliman   Hey — what odds you offerin', Grib?

Gribble   Hundred to one our school to win. Fifty to one if we score a point. Twenty to one if the game finishes. Any of you guys want a piece of the action?

(Vigorous shaking of heads.)

Coach   Gribble, how dare you drum up business in here!

Gribble   Fat chance, sir. I haven't taken a single bet all day. Not even from the Saxby boys.

Coach   Haven't you? Well, just to show you that I have faith in you, I'm going to bet one dollar on the school to win. *(He takes a dollar from his pocket and hands it to the amazed* **Gribble***. The boys look at him with open mouths.)*

Brewster   Sir — you're crazy.

Coach   Am I? You see, *I* know when I'm on to a good thing. *I* know we can win. *(He pauses and looks around in triumph.)* Now — who's going to join me in a little bet?

(But again there is a mass shaking of heads – only more vigorous than before. **Gribble** *grins and pockets the money.)*

Gribble   Hey, Bailey, some of the junior kids are runnin' a book on which of ya gets carried off first. *You* got most of the bets.

Bailey   *(horrified)* Me? Why?

Gribble   You should see the Saxby lock.

Bailey   What's he really like, Grib?

Gribble   Like somethin' that come up out of the swamp — a million years ago. They reckon he doesn't talk — just grunts.

Phillips   Grunt, grunt — me hungry, me kill!

Bailey   Oh, gawd.

Coach   Gribble, you're an utter disgrace. Worse than that, you're a traitor. Now, get out!

Gribble   But sir, the headmaster said he wanted a full report — for the next of kin, sir.

Coach   Very well — but no more bets! Understand?

Gribble   Yes, sir. *(***Gribble** *gets his pad back and wanders to the right, again taking notes.)*

Coach   Right, now boys — let's cut this game down to the bare bones —

Bailey   Please, sir — don't talk about bones —

Coach Grow up, Bailey. I mean, let's look at their team and see if we can spot any weaknesses.

Gribble I've spotted one, sir.

Coach There, you see — they're not unbeatable. What is it, Gribble?

Gribble Well, sir, I've covered some of Saxby's games and they tire easily, sir. By half time they've had it.

Coach Is that a fact? Well, all we have to do is save ourselves —

Gribble A team gets pretty tired scoring twenty tries by halftime, sir.

Coach *(losing his temper)* Gribble! I warned you —

Gribble *(retreating)* Sorry, sir. Not another word sir.

Coach See you don't — Waite, stop fidgeting, boy, and listen!

Waite Sorry, sir.

Coach What've you got under your jumper?

Waite Just padding, sir.

Coach Padding? It looks more like a book. Give it here!

*(**Waite** pulls it from under his jumper and passes it across. The **Coach** stares at it.)*

Did you really *have* to choose the Book of Common Prayer, Waite?

Waite I thought it might be a comfort, sir. I know a couple off by heart. How's this one? *(He recites.)*

'The Lord is my shepherd
I shall not want.
He maketh me to lie down in green pastures.'

Boys *(as one)* Amen.

Bailey I don't think I like the bit about lyin' down in green pastures.

Brewster Sorta like a cemetery, ain't it?

*(The **Coach** throws his hands in the air in disgust.)*

Coach What's the use? I feel like giving up —

Brewster Then the game's off, sir? Right, you guys, back to school —

(A mass movement for the door. But the **Coach** *finds new resolution — from somewhere.)*

Coach   No, it's not! Never! You'll play this game if it kills you!

Bailey   Oh, sir — please don't talk about —

Coach   I know, I know. All right, Bailey. Come on, boys, sit down.

(Slowly they do so.)

Now, listen — Saxby has a good set of forwards. They're heavy, but slow. *(He turns so that he addresses the boys on his right.)* It's up to you forwards to hold them, block them down the middle, tackle them right out of the game —

Brewster   Er . . . couldn't the backs look after that, sir?

Soliman   *(alarmed)* You're joking, Brewster!

Coach   The backs! And what will you lot be doing?

Brewster   I thought we might just jog up an' down the field for a bit. You know, show off the clean gear —

Coach   *(fiercely)* You get in there and knock them over! Remember, the bigger they are, the harder they fall.

Murphy   They'll pro'bly fall over our bodies.

Coach   Bailey, their lock is big and tricky so you'll have to watch him.

Bailey   I'm long sighted, sir, so I'll have to watch him from a fair way off —

Coach   You hit him, boy, hit him early and hard!

Phillips   That's what the Marsden lock did, sir — hit him early and hard.

Coach   And what happened?

Phillips   The Saxby lock got mad an' ripped his whole skin off — screeeep! He sorta just folded up — glop! They took him away in a bucket.

Bailey   I feel ill. I think I'm coming down with diphtheria.

Coach   Murphy, you're the hooker, so make sure their hooker doesn't get away with anything in the scrums.

Soliman   Yeah — like ya head, Murph.

Murphy   Belt up, Soliman!

*(The **Coach** now turns his attention to the backs, on his left.)*

Coach   If you're going to play halfback, Soliman, you've got no time for jokes. It's up to you to get the ball out to the backs.

Soliman   *(dismayed)* The ball, sir? I was hopin' I wouldn't see too much of the ball, sir.

Shaw   No need to get it out to us, Soliman — you keep it to yourself.

Allen   Yeah — we don't want the rotten thing.

Tulley   Why don't ya give it back to the forwards?

Murphy   That's a dumb idea, Tulley — we don't want it.

*(With a heavy sigh, the **Coach** presses relentlessly on.)*

Coach   Shaw, hit their five-eighth hard.

Shaw   I'd rather not, sir . . . if you don't mind.

Coach   Why, for heaven's sake?

Shaw   He might get upset.

Phillips   Screeep — off comes ya skin! Sprong — yer a little red heap!

Coach   Shut up, Phillips! Now you centres, run hard and straight —

Brewster   For *their* line, this time, Allen, not ours.

Coach   Quiet! Grant, you take all the kicks —

Grant   Who from, sir?

Coach   The kicks at goal, stupid. Tremain, as fullback, you're our last line of defence. I don't want a repetition of the Marsden game when you tried to hide behind the goalpost.

Tremain   I was lookin' for my contact lens, sir.

Coach   Now boys — are there any last requests — I mean, questions?

Brewster   One sir.

Coach   Yes, Brewster?

Brewster   Can we forfeit, sir?

*(The **Coach** suddenly changes his whole tone.)*

Coach   Boys, I know you're not looking forward to this. Believe me, if I could I'd change places with one of you right now —

(Thirteen hands shoot up.)

No, no, no — I don't want volunteers. Jokes aside, boys. All I want you to do is to try. I've put a lot of work into you. I know you can't beat the world — but you can do your best. If you do, then I'll be proud of you.

Brewster   And we'll all be buried with full military honours.

Team   *(in unison)* Amen.

(The piercing sound of a whistle is heard from outside. The team reacts as though sentence has finally been pronounced.)

Coach   There's the whistle. Brewster, lead your men out. Get out there, boys, and . . . and . . . well, good luck.

Gribble   Sir?

Coach   Yes, Gribble? *(He crosses to **Gribble**. Behind him, the team has not moved.)*

Gribble   What d'ya want me to do with the first-aid kit, sir?

Coach   What's in it?

Gribble   *(grinning)* Four miles of bandage, five thousand pain killers — and a white flag, sir.

Coach   *(wearily)* Just leave it there, Gribble — and go away.

Gribble   Sorry, sir. *(But **Gribble** remains.)*

*(The **Coach** turns back to his team and is somewhat surprised to find that they have not moved. But he is moved — to exasperated anger.)*

Coach   What are you lot still doing here? Get moving before I go out there and take Saxby on myself —

Brewster   *(hopefully)* Would you, sir? Right you guys, back to school —

(This time they do move.)

Coach   *(wearily)* Please go, boys. Just — try.

*(Their backs against the wall, the boys shamble out, except **Gribble** and the **Two Reserves**.)*

Gribble   Aren't you goin' to sit on the sidelines, sir — with the Saxby coach?

Coach   No. *(He slumps on the bench.)*

Gribble   Can't bear to watch, sir?

Coach   I can't bear to watch you, Gribble.

Brooks   D'ye mind if we reserves stay too, sir?

Coach   No, but stick around. You'll probably be needed.

Brooks   In here, sir?

Coach   No — out on the field, idiot.

(There is a roar from the crowd outside.)

Gribble   The game's about to start. I'll bring you a running report, sir. *(He rushes out.)*

*(The crowd noise dies down. There is a long silence as the **Two Reserves** come over and sit beside their **Coach**, whose head is hanging low.)*

Rankin   Don't let him get to ya, sir.

Coach   Who? Oh, Gribble. He's just a pest, that's all.

(A blast from a whistle, outside.)

Brooks   That's it! It's on!

*(There is another silence as all three strain to listen. A roar from the crowd makes them look at each other. **Gribble** runs in.)*

Gribble   Saxby's scored!

Coach   *(dismayed)* Already?

Gribble   It was our kick-off. Their lock caught the ball an' ran straight through. Scored under the posts without a hand laid on him!

Coach   Where were our forwards?

Gribble   Watching, sir.

Coach   And our backs?

Gribble   Watching too, sir. A couple of them gave him a clap.

*(The **Coach** groans deeply.)*

Bailey asked him for his autograph as he went past.

(Another groan, deeper and in pain.)

I'll go and see if he kicks the goal. *(He runs out.)*

Coach   *(weakly)* Just a lucky fluke! Our boys probably weren't ready . . .

Brooks   *(unconvinced)* Yes, sir.

(Another roar.)

I think they kicked it, sir.

Coach   *(sadly)* It seems so.

(There is an embarrassed silence.)

Rankin   Sir?

Coach   What, Rankin?

Rankin   We're gunna get done, aren't we, sir?

Coach   *(bravely)* Of course not.

Rankin   Sir! We're gunna get smashed. We knew that from the beginnin', didn't we?

Coach   *(sadly)* Yes — we knew. Only — we didn't admit it. You don't admit those things, you know, Rankin.

Rankin   But, sir — why did we bother with all the trainin' an' all the talkin'? It's like we been pretendin' all the time.

Coach   Rankin, it's not the winning that's important — it's how you play the game. It's . . . doing your best . . . putting on a good show . . . .

Rankin   Wouldn't ya like to win, though, sir — I mean deep down?

Coach   *(suddenly changing)* Yes, yes I would! I'd give anything to win! Just this once! Dear God, I would —

Brooks   I don't think prayin's gunna do any good, sir.

Coach   You're right, Brooks, you're right. What's the use? We're not going to win and it's all my fault. Where did I go wrong?

Brooks   Somewhere about the beginnin' of the season, sir.

Coach   But I taught you all the basics of the game. You can run, tackle, kick, pass the ball —

Rankin Yes, sir — but we're not much good at football.

*(A roar from the crowd and **Gribble** rushes in.)*

Gribble Saxby's in again! Ten nil an' they ain't even puffed!

Coach *(despairing)* What's going on out there?

Gribble Nothin' much, sir. The Saxby boys are standin' round tossin'
a coin to see who scores the next try. *(He runs out again.)*

Coach Ten nil in the first three minutes! What'll it be by halftime?

*(Silence. **Brooks** is figuring.)*

Brooks With forty minute halves, sir, it'll be about a hundred an'
thirty nil by halftime.

Coach The shame of it! Oh, the shame! Gribble was right — I'm a
coward — I can't bear to watch.

*(**Gribble** runs in. The **Coach** looks up again.)*

Again?

Gribble No, sir — reserve needed.

*(The **Coach** immediately leaps for the first-aid box.)*

Coach   Who's hurt?

Gribble   No one, sir. But Brewster's gone home.

Coach   He's what?

Gribble   Gone home, sir. He just ran off the field an' out through the gate.

Coach   I'll never face the headmaster. On you go, Brooks.

Brooks   *(jumping)* Me, sir? Couldn't Rankin —

Coach   You, Brooks!

Brooks   I'd just as soon stay, sir.

Coach   Move, boy!

(**Brooks** *starts to leave.*)

Gribble   Bye, Brooky.

Brooks   Bye, Grib. Bye, Rankin — you can have my stamp collection —

Coach   *(yelling)* Out!

(**Brooks** *runs out.*)

Gribble   Would ya rather I didn't bring any more news, sir?

Coach   *(sitting again)* No — I might as well know now as later.

Gribble   Right, sir.

(*A roar from the crowd.*)

Whoops — they're at it again!

(*He leaves. There is a long silence. The* **Coach** *hangs his head in despair.*)

Rankin   I . . . I suppose I'm next, sir.

Coach   Next?

Rankin   To go out there.

Coach   Oh. Yes, you are.

Rankin   We're pretty desperate, aren't we, sir — havin' to use me, I mean?

Coach   If you're trying to get out of it, Rankin —

Rankin   Oh no, sir — I'm not. Not really. I . . . sorta accept my fate. *(He takes a deep breath.)* But, sir — we both know what a hopeless footballer I am. I can't catch, I can't pass, I can't tackle. An' most of the time I've got a runny nose and the sniffles.

Coach   *(softened)* If I remember rightly, Rankin, you're a pretty hot tennis player, aren't you?

Rankin   *(embarrassed)* Yes, sir.

Coach   Then why play football? Do you like getting your body broken?

Rankin   No, sir. Actually . . . I'm scared stiff.

Coach   Then why play?

Rankin   Because . . . of you, sir.

(There is a long pause. The **Coach** *stares at him, amazed.)*

Coach   Me?

Rankin   Yes, sir. Most of the guys feel the same. *(Pause.)* Most of 'em would rather be playin' tennis.

Coach   But why me? You haven't won a game since I took over the team. I don't think you've even scored a point — except when you played the senior girls.

Rankin   You're the only one who'll coach us, sir.

Coach   That doesn't make any difference.

Rankin   It does to us, sir. It isn't your fault that we always lose. I just wish we could win — just once, because . . . that's what you want, sir. But we're lousy footballers.

Coach   *(smiling)* And that makes me a lousy coach, eh?

Rankin   I dunno, sir. *(Pause.)* I saw you cryin' when the senior girls beat us, sir.

Coach   I almost gave up right then.

Rankin   But you didn't did you, sir? You kept on tryin' even when the other teachers laughed at us — and at you. I saw 'em.

Coach   It was just a joke, Rankin.

Rankin   Some joke! Why don't you give us away, sir?

Coach   I don't really know. Perhaps I just hope that someday a miracle will happen — and we'll win.

*(A prolonged roar from the crowd. After a moment **Gribble** staggers in supporting a limping and battered **Murphy**. The **Coach** and **Rankin** spring to their feet.)*

Gribble   Second reserve on! *(He dumps the groaning **Murphy** on the bench.)*

Coach   What happened?

Gribble   Saxby gave him the ball an' Murph got crunched.

Coach   They gave him the ball? Why?

Gribble   Just their idea of a sick joke, sir.

Coach   On you go, Rankin.

Rankin   Where'll I play, Murph?

Murphy   Anywhere. You're the captain.

Rankin   Me?

Murphy   Yeah. Brewster made me captain. An' now I'm makin' you captain.

Rankin   Me? Captain? Wow!

Gribble   I'll show ya the way, Rankin — in case ya get lost. *(**Gribble** and **Rankin** run out.)*

Coach   Do you want the ambulance, Murphy?

Murphy   No, sir.

Coach   What's wrong, then?

Murphy   I think me body's broken, sir.

Coach   Which one of them got you?

Murphy   All thirteen — twice!

Coach   What happened?

Murphy   Well, sir — everythin' was goin' just great. They was just runnin' up an' down the field scorin' tries an' chattin' away an' we was just standin' around, sorta, clappin' with the crowd an' kickin' the ball to them. Then this mug lair of a Saxby captain comes up an' gives me the ball. Have a run, he says, laughin' so much he was chokin'. I looked around for someone to give the ball to but everyone was lookin' the other way. I was gunna throw the rotten thing away but the Saxby captain said he'd belt me if I did.

Coach   So what did you do?

Murphy   Hardly anythin' sir. I started this sorta slow trot an' then all the Saxby guys came up an' jumped up an' down on me . . .

Coach   Where's Brewster?

Murphy   Gone home, I think.

Coach   And how are the rest of the boys doing?

Murphy   Pretty good, sir. Though me havin' the ball scared 'em a bit.

Coach   What's the score?

Murphy   About twenty nil —

(Roar from the crowd.)

Twenty three nil. *(Pause.)* I think we're gunna lose this one, sir.

Coach   I think you're right. Never mind, Murphy, there's always a next time.

Murphy   *(pained)* Don't say that, sir.

Coach   Sorry. Well done, anyway —

(A tremendous roar from the crowd.)

Murphy   Listen to that! Either a five pointer or another crunchin'.

*(**Gribble** runs in. He stops short, his face wild with shock.)*

Coach   What is it, Gribble — another accident?

Gribble   No, sir . . . the game's over . . .

Coach   What! Don't tell me they've all gone home!

Gribble   No, sir . . . sir, we've won!

(A stunned silence.)

Coach   *(weakly)* We've . . . . what?

Gribble   Won, sir, won! We've beaten Saxby!

Coach   How?

Gribble   *(in a rush)* The ref disqualified Saxby for havin' fourteen men on the field! Rankin made him count 'em!

*(The **Coach** collapses on the bench, in disbelief.)*

Coach   We've won . . . we beat Saxby . . . a miracle . . . .

*(The team runs in, noisily chatting. As the last one enters, **Brewster** sneaks in behind, wearing a strange football jumper, his face muddy. Unseen he hurries to a locker and begins to put a coat on.)*

Rankin   Sir, sir — did ya hear?

Coach   *(sobered by now)* I heard.

Phillips   Our first win! All fair an' square! Wham! Bam! Boy, did we show 'em!

Bailey   Three cheers for the coach — hip, hip —

Coach   *(standing)* Boys, boys! This is no time for cheering.

(Instant silence.)
I'm happy we won but I'm not happy we won this way.

Phillips   Ah, sir — they deserved to lose. They cheated.

Coach   They made a mistake, Phillips. Why should they cheat when they probably could have beaten us with five men?

*(This immediately deflates the boys. But the **Coach** suddenly changes.)*

Still — we won! And that's something!

Boys   Yes, sir!

*(**Brewster** begins to sneak out as the boys become happy and noisy again. But the **Coach** sees him.)*

Coach   Brewster!

*(**Brewster** freezes. The boys spin around, suddenly silent.)*

What are you doing here? I thought you went home.

Brewster   I . . . sorta came back, sir.

Coach   Well, sorta get yourself over here, boy!

(**Brewster** *shuffles over, clutching his coat across the front. The boys are silent, anticipating a row.*)

What a mess! *(He peers closer.)* Open your coat.

(**Brewster** *slowly does so.*)

Brewster, you've got a Saxby jumper on!

Brewster   *(mumbling)* Yes, sir.

Coach   Where'd you get it?

Brewster   In the Saxby dressing room, sir.

Coach   What — a souvenir?

Brewster   No — er, yes, sir. That's it, sir, a souvenir.

Coach   They wouldn't give it to you — Brewster, you stole it!

Brewster   Yes, sir.

(*The* **Coach** *is seized with sudden suspicion — and horror.*)

Coach   When . . . did you steal it, Brewster?

Brewster   When I come off the field, sir.

Coach   Where did you go after that?

Brewster   *(brightly now)* Back on the field, sir.

Coach   *(horrified)* The fourteenth man . . . oh, my sainted aunt! Tell me it isn't true.

Brewster   Oh, it's true, sir. A bit of mud on me face an' no one noticed the difference. I even scored one of their tries.

Coach   But, but, but, but . . . but this makes us the greatest cheats in the history of football! Oh, dear merciful heavens . . . this is awful!

Brewster   I'm sorry, sir.

Coach   Sorry! *(He laughs hysterically.)* You've just conned a whole football team, a thousand spectators and a ref — and you're sorry!

Brewster   Yes, it is funny, isn't it, sir? *(He laughs too and soon the team joins in.)*

*(The **Coach** explodes in rage.)*

Coach   Stop it! Stop it! Have you no sense of right and wrong? Cheats, criminals . . . I've got to tell the Saxby coach . . . oh, the shame, the shame . . . *(He heads for the door but **Rankin's** voice pulls him up.)*

Rankin   Sir!

*(The **Coach** turns to him.)*

It isn't how you play the game, sir — it's the winning! And we won, sir — it's a miracle!

Coach   It's a scandal, that's what it is!

Rankin   No, sir, it isn't that. It's fair, in a sorta way.

Coach   Fair?

Rankin   Yes, sir. They laughed at us an' made fun of us an' you. An' they crunched Murph when there was no reason for it. *(Pause.)* An' we beat 'em, sir — boots an' all!

*(The **Coach** stares at them. They look up at him in dumb appeal, silently begging with forlorn eyes.)*

Coach   But how will I ever walk onto a football field again? How will I ever face people again? *(Pause.)* How will I ever stand up in church again?

Rankin   Sir — if God ever reffed a footie game, I reckon he'd let us win this one.

*(The **Coach** stares at **Rankin** in bewilderment — which shortly gives way to firm decision.)*

Coach   Yes, Rankin, I think He would. *(He comes back.)* Yes, indeed — we did it, boys — we beat Saxby, fair and square . . . in a sorta way.

*(The boys cheer. The **Coach's** spirits rise.)*

Drinks for everyone!

(Another cheer.)

But first!

(Sudden silence.)

Gribble!

Gribble   Yes, sir?

Coach   You owe me exactly one hundred dollars.

Gribble   One hundred — ah, sir, I was only kiddin'. . .

Coach   A bet is a bet, Gribble.

Gribble   Okay, sir. I'll pay you right after I print my story tomorrow. *(He pauses significantly.)* The *whole* story.

*(In horror, the boys look to the **Coach** — but he is equal to the occasion.)*

Coach   Can your silence be bought, Gribble?

Gribble   *(brightly)* Oh, yes, sir.

Coach   For how much?

Gribble   Exactly one hundred dollars, sir.

(*The boys cheer.*)

Coach   Come here, Brewster. Get that jumper off and burn it! Then we'll discuss plans for the return match against Marsden!

(*Prolonged cheering.*)

CURTAIN

Questions

1 As the play opens, the coach is trying to instil courage and confidence into the boys. How do they react?

2 In what connection does the coach first use the phrase, 'boots an' all'?

3 What job does Gribble do (a) for the school?
                        (b) for himself?

4 How does he obtain the inside information necessary for both jobs?

5 In your opinion, what is the most horrible thing, according to rumour, that has been done by a Saxby player (or Saxby players) to an opponent?

6 When Saxby first scores, the coach finds out that his forwards and backs were not exactly in there tackling. What were they doing? What did Bailey do as the Saxby lock went past?

7 The coach bets a dollar on the school to win. What reason does he give for the bet?

8 'Most of the guys would rather be playin' tennis' says Rankin. Why are they in the football team?

9 What trick is finally used to beat Saxby?

10 Explain how the sum of $100 comes to be linked with the fact that the true story of the game is never printed.

Bonny Johnny

Larry Pigram

Cast

Compere
Man I
Bartender
Bonny Johnny
Doc
Man II
Settler
Cook
Indian
Man III
Hepatitis

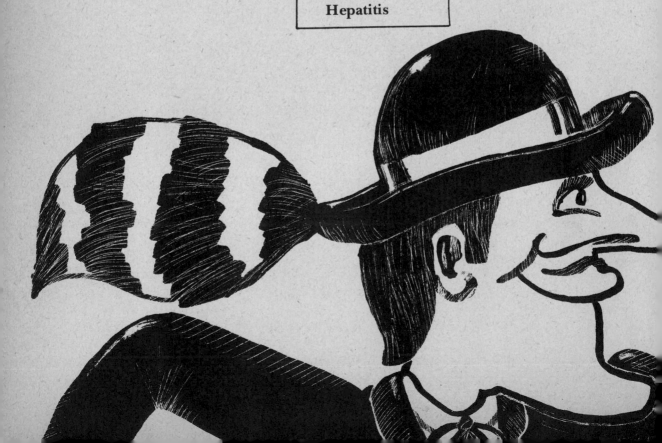

Compere In the past few years there has developed a new type of western hero. He is cultured, cool but quick tempered and above all he has a keen wit. We now present our own version of this hero. Here is Bonny Johnny!

(A typical western saloon. Numerous bystanders.)

Man I *(rushing in)* Look out everybody — it's Bonny Johnny, the meanest, dirtiest outlaw in all the west.

*(**Bonny Johnny** enters, wears morning suit, vest, cane, etc., also bowler hat, with raccoon tail on back — walks, to bar.)*

Bartender What'll it be Johnny?

Bonny Johnny The usual, thanks Cyril.

Bartender Okay, double Porphyry Pearl coming up.

Bonny Johnny I say, did you see my horse as I rode up.

Bartender Yep, Tinfoil's looking a little old on it, isn't he?

Bonny Johnny Whatta ya mean old?

Bartender Well, look at his long beard.

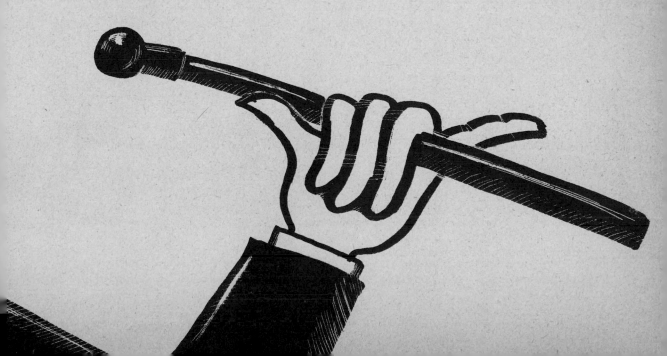

Bonny Johnny   You're looking at the wrong end, stupid. *(Pulls gun and shoots him — notches gun.)* If there's one thing I can't stand, it's a stupid bartender. *(To man.)* Take him up to Boot Hill.

Man I   Johnny, how come you always bury them at Boot Hill Cemetery.

Bonny Johnny   Well, sometimes because they're good, sometimes because they're bad, but mainly because they're dead.

Doctor   *(walks to bar)* Hi there, Johnny.

Bonny Johnny   Who are you?

Doctor   I'm the frontier doctor.

Bonny Johnny   Well, you can't get many patients.

Doctor   Why do you say that?

Bonny Johnny   Well, there aren't many people with front ears.

  (Goes into hysterics.)

Man I   Eh?

Bonny Johnny   *(still laughing)* Don't you get it? Frontier doctor — front e-a-r-s. Laugh you idiot! *(Pulls out gun — shoots him.)*

Doctor   Why'd you shoot him, Johnny?

Bonny Johnny   *(notching his gun)* Because I love peace.

Doctor   But you killed him.

Bonny Johnny   Well, there's nothing so peaceful as a dead man.

Man II   Hey Johnny. Did you know that doc was at Little Big Horn with Custer.

Bonny Johnny   You mean you were actually there when those cursed cows killed Colonel Custer?

Doctor   Yep.

Bonny Johnny   You mean you were there when those abysmal Apaches axed him in the abdomen?

Doctor   Yep.

Bonny Johnny   You mean . . .

Doctor   Ah, be quiet!

Bonny Johnny   Okay, Doc, how about a game of cards?

Doctor   Right, what do you prefer, poker, Blackjack?

Bonny Johnny   How about a few rounds of Whist or Old Maid?

> (**Settler** *staggers in, arrow jutting from his belly.*)

Bonny Johnny   I say, what happened to you?

Doctor   It looks like those baseless bounders have banged old Bob in the belly.

Bonny Johnny   You mean some galloping gourmet has got him in the gut?

Man II   You mean . . .

Settler   Ah, be quiet! Doc, doc, you got to help me.

Doctor   What is it, Bob?

Settler   Doc! Doc! Before I go, will you take a message to my Maw.

Doctor   Sure Bob, what is it?

Settler   *(gasping)* Tell her *(Cough)* — tell her *(Cough, cough.)*

Doctor   Yes man, quickly.

Settler   Tell her *(Cough, cough, cough.)*

Doctor   Yes.

Settler   Tell her . . . tell her . . . Ayee in . . . Ugh . . . *(Dies.)*

Doctor   What'd he say?

Bonny Johnny   Ay . . . ee . . . in . . . ugh . . .

Man II   What's that mean.

Bonny Johnny   I dunno . . . must be Maw's Code.

Man II   Eh?

Bonny Johnny   Don't you get it — Maw's Code? *(Shoots him.)* Laugh
you idiot. *(Notches his gun.)*

*(**Doctor** picks up **Settler's** wrist, feels for pulse — lets it drop with
a thump — pulls **Settler's** hat over his face.)*

Bonny Johnny   Will he live?

Doctor   Well, if he does, he'll be a pretty sick boy.

Bonny Johnny   You mean he's gone.

Doctor   Yes, gone. Gone to the Big Metro Goldwyn Mayer Western
Spectacular in the Sky.

Bonny Johnny   *(runs across the stage)* Well, I guess this looks like a job
for . . . Bonny Johnny!

Cook   Watch for this mighty leap onto his fiery steed.

Bonny Johnny   *(off stage)* Hi Ho, Tinfoil! *(A scream, then a thump is
heard. **Bonny Johnny** limps back in.)*

Doctor   You all right, Johnny?

Bonny Johnny   I'll live, but I'd sure like to get the varmint who
moved my horse.

Doctor   You mean some simpering sot has stolen your steed?

Cook   Yes, you mean some nattering nit has nicked off with your
nag?

Doctor You mean . . .

Bonny Johnny Ah, be quiet!

(**Indian brave** and **squaw** enter.)

Indian How! Me and my sister cold and hungry.

Bonny Johnny I see, you just dropped in to get your wig warm. (Goes into hysterics.)

Man III Eh?

Bonny Johnny (still laughing) Don't you get it? Wig warm . . . Wig w-a-r-m. (Pulls out gun — shoots him.) Laugh you idiot. Okav take him up to Boot Hill.

Indian What Boot Hill?

Doctor That's where we bury old boots.

Bonny Johnny Yeh, with the feet still in 'em.

Indian We want something to eat.

Cook Do you mind eating yesterday's corn hash?

Indian No.

Cook Good, well come back to-morrow.

Indian How you like to be burnt at stake?

Cook Okay, okay, don't get your loincloth in a knot.

Indian (to **Bonny Johnny**) Say, my sister like you.

Bonny Johnny Yeh? What's her name?

Indian Hepatitis.

Bonny Johnny Hepatitis? Say, I bet she's got an infectious personality. (Goes into hysterics.)

Cook   Eh?

Bonny Johnny   Don't you get it? Hepatitis . . . infectious personality. *(Shoots him.)* If there's one thing I can't stand it's a cook with no sense of humour.

Hepatitis   *(to **Bonny Johnny**):* How. Me think you're a smashing sort. Me want to kiss you.

Doctor   How?

Hepatitis   Me already know how . . . all I gotta do is catch him.

Bonny Johnny   Say, how'd you get out here in the west?

Hepatitis   I came out in a covered waggon.

Bonny Johnny   Well, looking at you I don't blame them for covering it. Say, what's that you've got in your hair?

Hepatitis   Buffalo grease.

Bonny Johnny   Well, stand over there . . . the wind's in my favour.

Indian   No need to resist . . . she very strong.

Bonny Johnny   So I've noticed.

   (Drums sound in the background.)

Indian   Sounds like a message.

Bonny Johnny   It is. It's a message from the Creek Indians.

Indian   What's it say?

Bonny Johnny   Tum titty, tum titty, tum, tum, tum.

Indian   What that mean?

Bonny Johnny   I dunno — it's all Creek to me. *(Goes into hysterics.)*

Indian   Eh?

Bonny Johnny Don't you get it . . . Creek Indians — All Creek to me. *(Shoots him.)* Laugh you idiot.

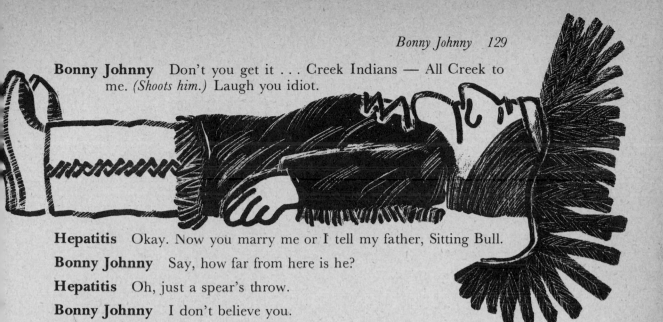

Hepatitis Okay. Now you marry me or I tell my father, Sitting Bull.

Bonny Johnny Say, how far from here is he?

Hepatitis Oh, just a spear's throw.

Bonny Johnny I don't believe you.

Hepatitis *(hands him spear)* Try it!

Bonny Johnny Okay. *(Throws spear — loud scream offstage.)* Okay, okay. I'll marry you.

Hepatitis Good. Here, you take my necklace.

Bonny Johnny Is it true your're the fattest squaw in all the west.

Hepatitis Yep, me only squaw who is six feet tall flat on back.

Bonny Johnny Well, that makes two horrible things that have come out west this year . . . and you're both of them.

Hepatitis Say, you better be nice to me or I'll take back my necklace.

Bonny Johnny Indian giver.

Doctor You'd better marry her, Johnny — you should have seen what happened to the other varmint who wouldn't marry her.

Bonny Johnny Yeh . . . where'd he get it?

Doctor Right in the teepee.

Bonny Johnny Wow! That's a pretty painful place to get it.

   (Goes into hysterics.)

Doctor Eh?

Bonny Johnny   Don't you get it? Teepee . . . Painful place to get it. *(Shoots him.)* Laugh you idiot!

Hepatitis   Oh, Johnny, I love you. You're so brave.

Bonny Johnny   Okay, okay. Let's go. *(Starts to pick his way through bodies.)*

Hepatitis   Say, Johnny, what do you think of my looks?

Bonny Johnny   Well, that's a nice dress you're almost wearing.

(Curtain begins to close.)

Hepatitis   Johnny, do you know how I can get rid of ten pounds of ugly, excess fat. *(Curtain still closing.)*

Bonny Johnny   Try chopping off your head. *(Goes into hysterics.)*

Hepatitis   Eh? *(Curtain almost closed.)*

Bonny Johnny   Don't you get it . . . ten pounds of excess fat . . . chop off your head. *(Curtain closes as shots are fired.)* Laugh you idiot . . . *(From behind curtain.)* Hi, ho, Tinfoil.

(Cast comes back to sing Finale.)

BONNY JOHNNY
(To the tune of 'Davy Crockett')

Raised by his mumma in Joe's cafe,
Poshiest place in the U.S. of A.
Shot my nappy full of holes one hot day,
'He's quick on the drawers', my mumma used to say.

CHORUS

Bonny, Bonny Johnny, king of the wild frontier.
My kindergarten teacher was good at her trade,
Best poker-player that ever was made.
But in her grave she was soon laid,
'Cause I caught her cheating at Old Maid.

CHORUS

While still fairly young I robbed a train
But Mumma said I would have to refrain,
As a killer I was always humane.
So I killed her with the minimum of pain.

CHORUS

Though I ain't mentioned my every detail,
There's something to see you could not fail.
I'm a true gentleman, hearty and hale,
I'm polished of boot and manicured of nail.
'Fore the most proper gent I would not pale
My hair always combed, my clothes never stale.
And at last when it's time to hit the trail,
Even old Tinfoil's got perfume on his tail.

Questions

1 Why are Bonny Johnny's jokes so deadly?

2 What reason does Bonny Johnny give for shooting
   (a) the bartender?
   (b) Man I?

3 What are the jokes that the doctor and Hepatitis fail to get?

4 There are some very funny pieces of alliteration (expressions in which the first letters of words are the same) in the play. Give three particularly funny examples.

5 What pun (play on words) does Bonny Johnny make about the name 'Hepatitis'?

6 What does Hepatitis think about Bonny Johnny?

7 What does Bonny Johnny think about Hepatitis?

8 How did Bonny Johnny first begin his shooting career?

9 To what extend does Bonny Johnny measure up to the Compere's description of the 'new type of western hero'?

10 What kind of humorous competition does Bonny Johnny occasionally engage in with the doctor and even with the cook?

A Modern Romeo and Juliet

Larry Pigram

Introduction

In 'Romeo and Juliet', the student is given the freedom to experiment with the script, if he so desires. The songs are not necessary to the script. However, much fun is produced for an audience if the actor mimes some of these songs. The student is not even compelled to use the same songs nominated in the script. A slight alteration in the words of the script will enable the student to use almost any song he wishes. 'She Taught Me to Yodel' produces a great response from the audience if the actor is prepared to gesticulate wildly. Even in the classroom situation, the records could be played if the teacher has them readily available.

Cast

Maxie Montague
Sylvie Montague
Romeo
Mercutio
Juliet
George Capulet

SCENE I

*This scene takes place in the Montague kitchen. The table is set for breakfast.
Corn Flakes, etc., are on the table.* **Sylvie Montague** *is seated, dressed in
Shakespearian garb.* **Maxie Montague** *enters.*

Maxie   Oh, alas and alack.

Sylvie   Maxie, Maxie, before thou bursts a gusset,
Pray, tell me what has made thee turn this shade of russet.

Maxie   *(he places his hand over his heart and indulges in various other theatrical
gestures)* Oh that on the morn of Romeo's return,
The fates have chosen me to spurn.
I am caught in their cruel mesh,
For some lousy dingo has stolen my 'Spray-Fresh'.

Sylvie   Fear not, Maxie, for from Flemings I have come,
And by chance brought with me an economy size 'Mum'.

Maxie   *(he pretends to be greatly relieved)* Although 'tis not the brand I
would chose,
I hope it's big enough for us both to use.

Sylvie   Oh, Maxie, thou art so romantic. *(She hugs him, but Maxie turns
away.)*

Maxie I couldst not be any other way for thou hast the face of a saint.
(Aside to the audience.) A St Bernard!

Sylvie Ohhhh, Maxwell.

Maxie Sylvie, thou art truly my saviour,
And I hope you will forgive my behaviour.
But I've just felt a suggestion,
Of another bout of indigestion.

Sylvie Oh, my poor dumpling.
But while you wait for this attack to blow,
Pray join me in a round of Montague a-go-go.

(Both of them go-go to go-go music. As they finish **Romeo** *enters.)*

Romeo Mother, Father, 'tis your son Romeo returned from his vacation,
With I might add a slight touch of palpitation.

Sylvie Maxie, 'tis our son Romeo returned from Switzerland and Surfers Paradise. *(They exchange greetings.)*

Romeo My dearest parents, you will be pleased to know that I have at last reached manhood. For while I was away I fell in love, with this beauteous little dove. **(Romeo** *goes out and brings in* **Juliet.)**

Juliet How do, Mr and Mrs Montague?

Maxie Romeo, Romeo, you know I always a sport have been,
But this little bird could not be more than fourteen.

Sylvie Maxie, do not fly into a rage.
Perhaps she looks young for her age.
And now, Romeo, while your father prays for help from above,
Pray tell us where you found your new love.

*(***Romeo** *mimes to 'I Lost My Heart in Hayman Island')*

Maxie She's truly beautiful, Romeo, and I can see how your passions she does rouse.
But won't you tell me the name of your new spouse?

Romeo Her name is Juliet Capulet, Father.

Maxie Capulet! But this cannot be.

Romeo   Why, Father?

Maxie   Oh, you cannot marry, you poor little fools.
You see, her father follows Aussie Rules.

Romeo   Oh, no.

Juliet   But what does this mean, Romeo?

Romeo   Oh, Juliet, Juliet, canst thou see by his face so lined with
fatigue,
That my father follows Rugby League?

Juliet   Oh, that the fates should throw up this cruel barrier,
Just when I shouldst choose to marry ya'.
Oh, Romeo. Good-bye. Our love cannot be,
For from you I must flee. *(**Juliet** rushes off, sobbing.)*

Romeo   Oh, no! *(He sits in the chair, then gets up and mimes 'Love Sick
Blues' or a similar song.)*

SCENE II

Two or three columns on the stage and a balcony.

Mercutio But Romeo, thou canst not forever go round the place,
With such a hang-dog expression on your face.

Romeo Mercutio, how could thou knowest? *(He places his hand over his heart.)*

Thou hast never been in love, with the sweetest flower that growest.

Mercutio To be, or not to be, that is the question.
Whether 'tis nobler in the mind to suffer the slings and arrows of outrageous fortune.

Romeo If you're wondering about the brevity of this act,
Or at a speech from Hamlet being in our play,
You must surely recognize the fact
That our writer could think of nothing else for us to say,
Therefore, as soon as Mercutio gives me the cue,
I'll have another song to sing for you.

Mercutio Romeo, won't you tell me whilst thou art with me standin'
Why you love Juliet with such abandon?

Romeo You see the reason she causest my blood to roar,
Is that she taught me something I never could do before.

Mercutio Pray, tell me what it is.

Romeo She taught me to yodel. *(He mimes to the song, 'She Taught Me to Yodel'.* **Mercutio** *leaves* **Romeo** *to his thoughts.* **Juliet** *appears on the balcony.)* But soft, what light through yonder window breaks?

Juliet Romeo, Romeo, wherefore art thou, Romeo?

Romeo I am here, Juliet, in my shoes of vinyl,
To take you to see the Grand Final.

Juliet Oh Romeo, my love, I canst not go with you.

Romeo Why not?

Juliet Another thing has come up to thwart our love, I fear.
I have something to tell you, my dear,
Which will no doubt your heart shatter.
You see, my love, I support Parramatta.

Romeo Oh no, not another barrier to forge.
(Aside.) You see, I support St. George.
But come, sweet light of my heart,
Let us kiss once before we part.

*(**Juliet** climbs down from the balcony and kisses **Romeo** in no uncertain manner.)*

Juliet Oh, Romeo, my love, do not come to me any more.

Romeo Why not?

Juliet People will say we're in love. *(She mimes to the song 'People Will Say We're In Love' and then she faints.)*

Romeo Oh, what have I done to this poor miss,
With the passionate power of my kiss?
But if, alas, my darling Juliet is gone,
I myself cannot go on.

*(Enter **Mr and Mrs Montague** with **Mr Capulet**.)*

Maxie So you see, George, if you allow my Romeo to wed Juliet,
It will end the feud between the Montagues and the Capulets.

George But how can I let my daughter wed this prawn,
Who follows a game of beef and brawn?

Sylvie But if you think the game smells so,

Why does your daughter to rugby go?
But what is this? Our children dead? *(She swoons. Then* **George**
examines her.)

Maxie   George, fear not. The sight has merely shocked her.
But post-haste get the doctor. (**George** *leaves.* **Sylvie** *wakes up a
few moments later.)*

Sylvie   But, Maxie, it is not within anybody's power
To get a doctor out of bed at this hour.

Maxie   But I have influence.

Maxie   Yes, influence. (**Maxie** *mimes to the song 'Influence'.* **George**
re-enters.)

George   Maxie, I fear the doctor cannot come.

Maxie   Why not?

George   When I arrived there, the lousy dingo,
Had gone out for a game of bingo.

Sylvie   It matters not. See, our children stir.

Romeo   Mother!

Sylvie   Romeo!

Maxie   By the fur on a sow's ear.
Pray, tell us what happened here.

Romeo   Father, father, I will tell you anon.
Just try and keep your shirt on.
You see, I have decided to wed my Juliet.

Juliet   Oh, Father, it worked.

Romeo   What dost this mean?

Juliet   When I was young, my father told me something on which to
ponder.
You see, he always believed that absence makes the heart grow
fonder.

Maxie   Romeo, my son. It was only a trick by Juliet's father.

Romeo   I care not. For because of our love so rare *(He grasps* **Juliet's**
hand.)
I will wed my lady fair.

Maxie But it's a scandal!

Sylvie Yes, a scandal! *(All the cast mime to 'It's a Scandal'.)*

Questions

1 What is it that is worrying Maxie as the play opens?

2 Name three extremely un-Shakespearian products mentioned in the first few lines of the play.

3 'Oh, that the fates should throw up this cruel barrier!' What is the cruel barrier?

4 What other objection does Maxie have to Juliet?

5 Why does Romeo *really* love Juliet?

6 Part of the humour of the play occurs when quite different words rhyme at the ends of lines. Give three startling pairs of rhyming words.

7 Why is it impossible for the doctor to attend those who have fainted?

8 What does Romeo finally decide to do about Juliet?

9 What old proverb did Juliet put into practice to capture Romeo?

10 In Shakespeare's play, the love between Romeo and Juliet was treated seriously. List the methods used by Pigram to make the love affair humorous.

The Raft

Richard Parker

Cast

Shipwrecked sailors:
    Corkie
    Dave A boy, very excitable
    Blondie A Cockney
    Pedro An Italian
    Joe A Cockney, treacherous
    A Man

Properties
    A raft
    A dagger
    A bucket
    A shovel
    Ragged and torn clothes
    A black eye-patch

SCENE

A raft on the open sea.

An empty stage in the centre of which is the raft. Small chest or box on the raft, a mast in the centre.

Joe   Ladies and gentlemen, it is important that you understand the scenery for this play. In the centre *(indicates)* you see a raft. All round it is the deep sea. Everywhere, except on the raft, is water as far as the horizon. This is very important. It is also very wet.

(He turns and waves right and left and the actors shuffle on self-consciously. They take their places on the raft. **Joe** *whispers in* **Blondie's** *ear and he nods, takes a black patch out of his pocket and adjusts it over his eye.* **Joe** *takes his place and there is silence for a while. The five men on the raft now look exhausted, as if they had been at sea for a considerable time.* **Joe***, dark, shifty-eyed, sits cross-legged, left.* **Pedro***, an Italian, small, wiry and given to sudden gesticulation, is lying full-length on one elbow, right.* **Blondie***, a giant of a man with almost white hair and a black patch over one eye, stands extreme right of raft and scans the horizon.* **Corkie***, older than the others, bearded and with an artificial leg, sits centre, his back to the mast, one leg straight out before him and the other doubled up.* **Dave***, a boy, is fishing over the back of the craft with his back to the audience. He hauls in his line and inspects it.)*

Corkie   *(without looking round)* Any luck?

Dave   Not yet. *(Throws line back in.)*

(This should be played very deliberately, even, for the first five or six speeches, letting the pace deliberately drag.)

Blondie   Not yet? You won't never catch anything like that.

Dave   *(suddenly angry, not loudly but suppressed)* You have a go then, if you know so much about it.

Blondie   I wouldn't waste my time, Dave boy. How can you catch fish without bait? You've been dangling that bit of string over-board for nearly two days now and what have you caught? Nothing.

Corkie   Leave the kid alone, Blondie. He's only trying to help.

Blondie   Well, why don't he put some bait on his hook? Then he might get something.

Dave   How can I put bait on when we finished our last crumb of food two days ago?

Blondie   Doesn't have to be food, does it? Borrow one of Pedro's socks; that ought to be nice and tasty. Might catch a whale with that.

Pedro   Very funny man, Mr Blondie. Make us all laugh ha-ha, yes? *(Leans forward with menace.)* You make another joke about my feet and I slit your throat for you, just you see if I don't.

Blondie   You? You couldn't slit a rice pudding. (Petro *draws his knife.*) Put that penknife away — you might cut yourself.

Corkie   You didn't ought to tease him, Blondie. You know he's got no sense of humour. Anyway, his socks wouldn't be no good for bait.

Blondie   Why's that, Corkie?

Pedro   All listen very hard now for big joke.

Corkie   They'd poison the water.

*(All laugh. **Pedro** half rises with knife up, as if to strike at **Corkie**. **Blondie** grabs his wrist, takes knife and pushes **Pedro** back.)*

Blondie   Sit down, mug.

Pedro   Oh, you break my arm, I think. *(Nurses his arm.)*

Blondie   I said you'd get hurt if you kept playing with that knife. I'd better keep it for you.

Pedro   But my arm, she is broke.

Corkie   Oh, pipe down.

*(A pause. **Dave** draws his line in again.)*

Corkie   Any luck?

Dave   Not yet.

Joe   *(jumps to his feet)* Talk, talk, talk. Natter, natter, natter. You're like a lot of old women. We've been on this perishing raft for five days now and all you've done is talk. To hear you anyone would think we was a Women's Institute out on a picnic. Don't you realise we've got no grub and no water? Don't you understand that if we're not picked up some time today we'll be finished?

Corkie   All right, Joe. Keep calm about it. You won't do no good arguing the toss.

Dave   We were lucky to get away from the wreck at all, if you ask me. What about all the rest of the chaps going down with the ship?

Joe   Well, it hasn't done us much good, has it? I'd sooner be drowned than die of thirst, and that's a fact. Have you ever seen a bloke that's died of thirst? Well, I have. All black and burnt up like a cinder, with his tongue all swollen up and stuck to his lips . . .

Blondie   All right, Joe. We know. It don't make it any better.

Joe   If only it would rain a bit.

Corkie   Well, it's not going to do that. Look at the sky.

Pedro   Plenty of water all round if you so thirsty.

Dave   Of course there is. Why didn't we think of that before?

(He scoops sea-water in his hands and drinks it.)

Corkie   Don't drink that, Dave boy.

Dave   Why not? It's good.

Blondie   Because it'll send you mad, that's why.

Dave I don't believe it. *(Drinks more.)*

Corkie Dave! Leave it alone! Stop him, someone!

Joe Oh, let him be. What difference does it make?

Corkie Dave! Stop it, I say! Ain't no one going to stop him?

Dave You leave me alone.

Corkie *(gets awkwardly to his feet and pulls* **Dave** *back from the edge of the raft)* You young fool. You don't know what you're doing.

Dave Stop ordering me about. I'm not a kid any more.

Corkie You don't know what you're doing, son. Salt water's poison. With a sun like this sitting on the back of your neck you'd go crazy in no time.

Dave What do I care? Joe's right. We'll all be dead by tomorrow anyway.

*(**Corkie** sits down. Despondent silence.)*

Pedro Isn't it time one of you funny English made another joke?

Blondie Shut up, Pedro. Here though, isn't it about your turn to look-out? I've been standing here all the morning.

Pedro It is my turn, maybe.

Blondie Good. Up on your feet then, sailor.

Pedro Too comfortable here.

Blondie You can't keep a lookout when you're lying down.

Dave I wish I had some shade. My head's burning.

Pedro Then I no keep lookout.

Blondie But you just said it was your turn. What the . . .

Pedro Blondie, you worry too much. You never grow to be an old man.

Blondie We've got to keep a lookout.

Corkie Oh, leave it, Blondie. What does it matter. Joe's right, I reckon. What's the use of anything?

Blondie Well, you may have given up, but I haven't. If you're all too lazy to stand up, I'll do it.

Pedro   Well said, Mr Blondie. You brave, good man. I love you. If you bend down I kiss you on both cheeks.

Blondie   Oh, shut up.

Pedro   Hey, Blondie!

Blondie   What is it now?

Pedro   Come a little closer over by here, please.

Blondie   Why?

Pedro   If you must stand up it's a pity to waste such shade. You stand just here and keep me cool.

Dave   Shade? I could do with some shade. Inside my head it's like a frying-pan.

Corkie   Never mind, son. Bear up.

Dave   *(in a quiet, strange voice)* But why don't we sail over there? Just under that big tree? Lots of shade there.

Joe   Tree? He's going crazy.

Corkie   Shsh! *(Gently.)* What tree, son?

Dave   *(pointing)* That oak tree over there.

Corkie   That's not a tree, Davie boy. Here, you lie down and have a little rest. Put your head in my shade. That's the idea. Get a bit of sleep. **(Dave** *lies down.)*

Pedro   And you shade me, good, brave Mr Blondie.

Blondie   You go to blazes.

Joe   What wouldn't I give for a pint of beer just now.

Corkie   Now you've said it. *(Wipes his lips.)*

Pedro   You English and your beer. I would have a glass of wine with tiny bubbles coming up from the bottom. My grandfather, now. He make a wonderful wine.

Corkie   Cut it out, Pedro. Only makes it worse for us. How long do you reckon we can last without a drink, Blondie?

Blondie   Hard to say. Not much longer, anyway. Tomorrow we shall all be so dry we shan't none of us be able to talk.

Joe   That'll be a blessing anyway.

Corkie   Seen anything yet?

Blondie   Not a thing.

Corkie   Suppose you do see a ship. Doesn't mean they'll see us, does it?

Pedro   Mr Blondie, he so clever he sure to think of something.

Blondie   Look Pedro. If you can't say nothing sensible you'd best keep your trap shut.

Pedro   Why? Shut *my* trap, no? Everybody else make noise but Pedro. He no can make noise, eh?

Blondie   If you know what's good for you . . .

Dave   *(cutting in)* What's all the fuss about? Have you seen something, Blondie?

Blondie   No, son. Nothing. You lie down and have a bit of shut-eye.

Dave   No, you're keeping something from me.

Corkie   Don't get yourself worked up, Davie boy.

Dave   I want to have a look for myself. *(Stands rather weakly and looks around.)* What have you seen? Where is it?

Blondie   I haven't seen nothing. Nothing but the perishing sea.

Dave   There it is! I knew you were keeping something from me.

Corkie   What's the kid seen?

Joe   *(jumping up)* Where is it, Dave?

Dave   Look! Out there! Coming this way. *(Points.)*

Joe   I can't see nothing.

Blondie   Course you can't. There's nothing to see.

Dave   *(insistent, excited)* But there is, I tell you. Have you all gone blind? It's a ship. Look! And she's coming towards us.

Corkie   *(now standing)* Where? Where?

Dave   Out there! She's coming about. She's lowering a boat.

Blondie   He's gone off his nut.

Corkie   Better lie down again, Dave. There ain't nothing there.

Dave   Take your hands off me. She's coming! She's coming! *(Cheers wildly and runs to the left side of the raft.)* All right, brother! Throw us your painter! *(Goes through the motions of catching a rope and tying up to the raft.)* Come on you chaps, we're saved.

*(No one moves. **Pedro** looks up and then lies down again with a groan.)*

Dave   Don't you want to be saved?

Corkie   It's no good, Dave. There's nothing there. You're just seeing things.

Dave   Don't come near me! Have you all gone mad? Well, you can stay here if you like. I'm going in the boat. Make room there, you chaps, I'm coming in!

Corkie   Hold him, someone. He'll drown himself in a minute.

*(**Blondie** moves towards **Dave**.)*

Dave   Keep away! Don't touch me! You shan't stop me.

Corkie   Grab him, Blondie.

Joe   Quick!

Dave   No! Wait for me! I'm coming.

(He runs across the raft and leaps clear so that he disappears in mid leap off the set.)

Corkie   Someone go in after him! You know I can't with this leg.

>   (**Blondie** *takes his jacket off.*)

Joe   Wait, Blondie! See that shark's fin?

Blondie   There's a dozen of them. That big one's right on him now.

>   (*A short, choked cry from* **Dave**, *off.*)

Corkie   *(turning away)*   Poor kid. Someone ought to have stopped him.

Joe   We tried, didn't we?

Blondie   Why didn't you?

Corkie   You know I can't move about with this leg. One of you could have grabbed him. We didn't ought to have just let him jump like that.

Pedro   *(looking up)*   What happen? Why you all make such noise? Where's Dave?

>   (*All silent.*)
>
>   Where's he gone? Why you no tell me?

Corkie   He went overboard, Pedro.

Pedro   Overboard? How was that? Someone push him, eh?

Joe   He jumped off. He was off his rocker, poor kid.

Blondie   Thought he saw a boat.

Pedro   Off his rocker? How does that mean?

Corkie   Mad, crazy. It was that salt water he drank. I told him not to drink it, didn't I? You heard me tell him?

Joe   All right, Corkie. Don't take it so bad. We heard you tell him.

Blondie   Course you did. It wasn't your fault, Corkie.

Corkie   Who said it was? It was your fault. You ought to have stopped him.

Blondie   Who? Me? I like that. Who was going to dive in after him?

Pedro   You all murderers. All of you. Why you make so much noise about it? You all talk and nag till poor boy he go crazy. I think I go crazy too if someone don't shut up.

Blondie   Why you . . . Who told the kid to drink sea-water in the first place? You, wasn't it? You're the one that started all this. Don't you call any of us murderers, you miserable little Dago, or I'll pick you up and throw you in there after him. You're the murderer, and don't you forget it.

Pedro   You think because you're so big and strong you can say anything, is that it? *(Gets menacingly on hands and knees and crouches ready for spring.)* Well, you not too big for me. You take that back or I think I kill you.

Blondie   *(backs to the edge of the raft and pulls out knife)* Don't forget I've got this now. You'd better lie down again before I lose my temper. If you come any nearer I'm liable to do something I'd be sorry for.

Pedro   *(deliberately)* You-fat-English-pig! I get you for this.

*(**Pedro** begins to move very slowly and menacingly across the raft towards **Blondie**. He is tensed and crouches slightly.)*

Voice off *(imperiously, very loudly)* Joe! Joe!

(All hold their positions but slowly turn their heads in the direction of the voice.)

Joe   *(in an ordinary voice, no longer the treacherous sailor, urgently)* Hold it a minute, you chaps! *(Meekly.)* Yes, Dad.

*(The others still hold their positions while **Joe** climbs down off the raft and stands waiting, watching the **Man** who now enters. This **Man** is in his shirtsleeves, carries a bucket in one hand and a shovel in the other. He walks up to the raft.)*

Man   Look, nip round next door and ask Mrs Robinson if she'll let us have a bucket of coke for the boiler.

Joe   Yes, Dad. *(Takes the bucket and shovel.)*

Man   And look sharp about it. *(**Joe** goes.)* It's nearly tea-time and I want all this mess cleared up before you finish out here. Where's Dave?

(They now, all together, relax their positions which should have been, until now, absolutely unmoving.)

Corkie   He was eaten by a shark.

Man   Then he'd better get uneaten, because I want him to go down to the shops before they close and get me a packet of fags.

END

Questions

1 What is the purpose behind Joe's coming on at the start of the play to speak to the audience?

2 Explain how the sailors come to be on the raft in the middle of the ocean.

3 Why does Blondie take a second turn as lookout man?

4 What are the first signs that Dave is starting to crack up, after he has drunk the salt water?

5 What stops the others from trying to rescue Dave after he jumps into the sea?

6 Explain why the bad feeling exists between the other sailors and Pedro.

7 Which character appears to be the most sensible person? Give some reasons for your choice.

8 The conflict in *The Raft* comes from the relationships between the characters. Between which characters does most of the conflict arise?

9 Write three sentences commenting on the speech of characters in *The Raft*. Note particularly any unusual qualities, and any differences between characters.

10 Is the surprise ending effective? Explain your feelings about the ending.

The Battle for Hopeless High

Larry Pigram

Introduction

This particular script should appeal to most high school students. With a little ingenuity, it can quite easily be adapted to fit a particular school and particular teachers. Names such as 'Numberstein', 'Killjoy', 'Bashwell', 'Baby Face' and 'Mr Jazz' together with the characteristics that go with them, can be altered to suit the staff of a particular high school.

Cast

Announcer
Commanding Officer (C.O.)
Neapolitan Polo
Von Numberstein
Revolutionary
Pilot
Herr Hater
Headmaster

SCENE I

(A table where the C.O. and Polo are poring over a map. The backdrop is covered with inflammatory propaganda such as 'Von Numberstein is a fink', 'Mr Jazz wears long underwear', 'Make war, not love', 'It's not the school we hate, it's the principal of the thing', etc.)

Announcer Throughout the centuries an undeclared war has been waged between students and teachers and although there has never been any lack of fervour on either side, open hostilities have rarely broken out. We were wondering what would happen if war were declared at the typical Australian high school. To show you what it would be like, we now take you to the student revolutionary headquarters, where crack secret agent Neapolitan Polo is being briefed before he leads a division on a most dangerous mission.

C.O. Polo, your mission is of the utmost importance to the student revolutionary movement, so what I am about to tell you must not go beyond this room.

Polo Quite, Sir.

C.O. Now for your mission. Its code name is 'Operation B.B.' The ultimate objective is the capture of the teachers' most effective weapon, Mrs B. Bashwell.

Polo Oh, no, not Bulldog Bashwell.

C.O. Yes, Bulldog Bashwell. You must avoid physical contact at all costs — use a net. Don't forget it's rumoured she makes her own alligator handbags.

Polo Sir, have you ever been in a battle against her?

C.O. Well, I once risked a verbal encounter with her.

Polo What happened?

C.O. Words flailed me.

Polo I see. As I've never seen Mrs Bashwell, sir, what's the first thing I'll notice about her?

C.O. That all depends on what direction she's facing.

Polo Quite. Now what about the route we're taking?

C.O.   Well, first you'll travel under the boys' toilet, across the girls' play-ground and into the headmaster's office. By the way, if you happen to find some canes in there, burn them. It'll demoralize him.

Polo   But sir, the language staffroom is just across the corridor. What will we do about Mr Killjoy?

C.O.   Oh, yes, Mr Killjoy. I'll arrange for Intelligence to steal his braces. He won't be chasing anybody.

Polo   Ingenious!

C.O.   Now in the headmaster's office, I want you to pile up the TV sets and joke books, then bore a hole through the roof into the music room. Oh, yes, you'd better look out for Mr Jazz. He may be small, but he's deadly with the symphony or the concerto.

Polo   Sir, what if we're captured by Von Numberstein or someone else from the maths staff gestapo.

C.O.   Under no circumstances tell them anything. Remember, all you have to tell them is name, rank, and desk number.

Polo   But what about Baby Face . . . One of the men is bound to crack under interrogation. I've heard about the things she does with the slide rule.

C.O.   I'm afraid you'll have to risk it.

Polo   Quite, sir.

C.O.   Now after leaving the music room cross to the English staffroom. Then rush in and grab Mrs Bashwell and parachute through the staffroom window. Have any of your men had parachuting experience?

Polo   No, sir.

C.O.   Very well. We'll train them in three stages. The first week we'll separate the men from the boys, the second week the boys from the idiots and the third week, we'll let the idiots jump.

Polo   Right, sir.

C.O.   Okay, Polo. Good luck. Now before you go, one last salute.

Both   Students of the world, unite!

    (Blackout.)

SCENE II

(The scene is basically the same, except that swastikas and Nazi emblems decorate the walls. The desk now has a lamp on it for interrogation purposes.)

Announcer   We now take you to the teachers' headquarters where the dreaded Von Numberstein is about to interrogate a revolutionary just brought in for questioning.

Von Numberstein   Okay, sonny, when did our men get you?

Revolutionary   A few minutes ago. I held up the school canteen with a sawn-off shotgun.

Von Numberstein   How come you were caught?

Revolutionary   I'd sawn off the wrong end.

Von Numberstein   Okay, let's have a look at your record. It says you assaulted a teacher when you were fourteen. Why?

Revolutionary   He called me a sissy.

Von Numberstein   And what did you do?

Revolutionary   I hit him with my handbag.

Von Numberstein   Hmmm. It says here you robbed the school canteen at fourteen and you assaulted the headmaster at fourteen. It also says you were expelled from school. When was this?

Revolutionary   When I was fourteen.

Von Numberstein   *(Grabbing the reading lamp and shining it in the Revolutionary's face.)* You dirty punk. Have you never done a good deed in your life?

Revolutionary   *(recoiling)* Well once I helped an old lady across the street.

Von Numberstein   What happened?

Revolutionary   She was hit by a bus.

Von Numberstein   Listen, sonny. How would you like a touch of the slide ruler?

Revolutionary   You don't frighten me, Numberstein.

Von Numberstein   Then how about a wrestling match with Mrs Bashwell?

Revolutionary   Oh, no, not with Bulldog, anything but Bulldog Bashwell.

(Blackout and a change back to the first scene.)

SCENE III

Announcer   We now take you back to the student revolutionary head-quarters where a pilot, who has been missing for four days, is being quizzed by the C.O.

C.O.   But how could it take you four days to drop a million propaganda leaflets over enemy territory?

Pilot   Oh, did we have to drop them? I thought we had to slip them under every door.

C.O.   Now, listen, Lieutenant, your morale had better improve. We're planning the big attack tonight, now that we've captured B.B. However, before you go, Lieutenant, there's something I want to ask you.

Pilot   What's that, Sir?

C.O.   I understand that four prisoners have escaped from your compound. Why?

Pilot   Well, I guess it was just a slip of the pen. But, anyway, I think I've got the prisoner who led the escapes. Come on in, Herr Hater.

   *(**Herr Hater** enters.)*

C.O.   What's your number, Herr Hater?

Herr Hater   863

C.O.   Oh, come on now, is that your real number?

Herr Hater   Well, no, not really, it's only my nick number.

C.O.   Now, Herr Hater, how did these men escape?

Herr Hater   I'm not goin' to tell you nothin'.

C.O.   How would you like to be sent down to Terrible Toby's torture room for a few minutes?

Herr Hater   Oh, no! You couldn't do it, the Education Department would never approve. You couldn't could you? *(The **C.O.** nods his head.)* All right, I'll confess.

C.O.   Okay. Do you admit that you and four other prisoners led an escape this morning?

Herr Hater Yes, yes.

C.O. And do you admit that you started a fight with a warder this morning?

Herr Hater Yes.

C.O. Why?

Herr Hater He called me a dirty number.

C.O. Okay. You're going back to the pen for another six-month term.

Herr Hater But, why? I've only just finished a six-month term.

C.O. Well, like I always said — one good term deserves another.

(Blackout.)

SCENE IV

Announcer We now take you to the teachers' headquarters where the headmaster is making a morale-boosting speech to his followers.

*(The **Headmaster** enters and gives the 'V' sign. The '1812 Overture' is heard in the background.)*

Headmaster   On May 13th, I asked the staff, which had been specially summoned, for a vote of confidence in the administration. After reporting the progress which had been made in filling the various staffrooms, I said I have nothing to offer but blood, toil, tears and sweat. In all our short history, never has a headmaster faced such a crisis as I do now. You ask what is our policy. I would say it is to wage war, that is our policy. You ask what is our aim. I can give one word, 'Victory'. *(Here he makes the 'V' sign.)* Victory at all costs. That is our aim. Even though large tracts of Hopeless High and many old and famous staff rooms have fallen, or may fall, into the hands of the students we shall not flag or fail, we shall go on to the end. We shall fight in the classrooms, we shall fight on the desk tops, we shall fight in the corridors, we shall fight in the staff rooms and on the stairs. We shall never surrender.

I expect that the battle of Hopeless High is about to begin. Upon this battle depends the survival of teacher administration. The whole fury and might of the students must very soon be turned on us. But the students know that they will have to break us in this office or lose the war. If we can stand up to them, all Hopeless High may be free. Let us therefore brace ourselves that if Hopeless High School and its staffrooms last for a thousand years — teachers will say, 'This was their finest hour.'

Questions

1   Why does everyone fear Bulldog Bashwell?

2   What joke in the play did you like best? Why?

3   What kind of a person is Von Numberstein?

4   What character do you like best in the play? Why?

5   How would you dress if you were playing the part of the C.O.?

6   Which scene do you think is the best? Why?

7   How would you play the part of the headmaster?

8   What scenery do you think would be needed for *Scene I*?

9   What evidence can you find to suggest that the headmaster of Hopeless High had an easy life before the revolution?

10   How is Herr Hater convinced to tell how the four prisoners escaped?

Noah

Andre Obey
(English Text by Arthur Wilmurt)

Cast	
Noah	The Bear
Mrs Noah	The Lion
Shem	The Monkey
Ham	The Elephant
Japheth	The Cow
Naomi	The Lamb
Sella	The Wolf
Ada	The Tiger
The Man	

SCENE ONE

A glade. The Ark is at the right, only the poop deck showing, with a ladder to the ground. **Noah** *is taking measurements and singing a little song. He scratches his head and goes over the measurements again. Then he calls:*

Noah *(softly)* Lord . . . *(Louder.)* Lord . . . *(Very loud.)* Lord! . . . Yes, Lord, it's me. Extremely sorry to bother You again, But . . . What's that? Yes, I know You've other things to think of, but after I've once shoved off, won't it be a little late? . . . Oh, no, Lord, no, no, no . . . No, Lord, please don't think that . . . Oh, but naturally, of course, I trust You! You could tell me to set sail on a plank — a branch — on just a cabbage leaf . . . Yes, You could even tell me to put to sea with nothing but my loincloth, even without my loincloth — completely — *(He has gone down on his knees, but he gets up immediately.)* Yes, yes, Lord, I beg Your pardon. I know Your time is precious. Well, this is all I wanted to ask You: Should I make a rudder? I say, a rudder . . . No, no, Lord, R for Robert; U for Una; D for . . . that's it, a rudder. Good . . . very good, I never thought of that. Of course, winds, currents, tides . . . What was that, Lord? Storms? Oh, and, while You're there, just one other little thing . . . Are You listening, Lord? *(To the audience.)* Gone! . . . He's in a bad temper . . . Well, you can't blame Him; He has so much to think of. All right; no rudder. *(He considers the Ark.)* Tides, currents, winds. *(He imitates the winds.)* Psch! . . . Psch! . . . Storms. *(He imitates the tempests.)* Vloum! Be da Bloum! Oh, that's going to be *(he makes a quick movement)* simply . . . magnificent! . . . No, no, Lord, I'm not afraid. I know that You'll be with me. I was only trying to imagine . . . Oh, Lord, while You're there I'd like just to ask . . . *(To the audience.)* Che! Gone again. You see how careful you have to be *(He laughs.)* He was listening all the time. *(He goes to the Ark.)* Storms! . . . I think I'll just put a few more nails in down here. *(He hammers and sings.)*

> When the boat goes well, all goes well,
> When all goes well, the boat goes well.

(He admires his work.) And when I think that a year ago I couldn't hammer a nail without hitting my thumb. That's pretty good, if I do say so myself. *(He climbs aboard the Ark and stands there like a captain.)* Larboard and starboard! . . . Cast off the hawsers!

... Close the portholes! ... 'Ware shoals! ... Wait till the squall's over! ... Now I'm ready, completely ready, absolutely ready! I'm ready. *(He cries to Heaven.)* I am ready! *(Then quietly.)* Well, I should like to know how all this business is going to begin. *(He looks all round, at the trees, the bushes, and the sky.)* Magnificent weather — oppressively hot and no sign of a cloud. Well, that part of the programme is His look-out.

*(Enter the **Bear**.)*

Well! ... What does *he* want?

*(The **Bear** moves towards the Ark.)*

Just a minute, there!

*(The **Bear** makes a pass at the Ark.)*

(Frightened.) Stop that. *(Pulls up ladder.)*

*(The **Bear** stops.)*

Sit down! Good.

*(**Bear** sits.)*

Lie down.

*(**Bear** lies down on its back and waves its legs gently.)*

There's a good doggie.

*(Enter the **Lion**.)*

What the devil!

*(The **Lion** puts its paw on the Ark.)*

None of that, you! . . . Lie down.

*(The **Lion** lies down beside the **Bear**.)*

Fine! . . . Splendid! . . . Now what do they want? Besides, why don't they fight? *(To the animals.)* Hey! Why aren't you fighting? Come on, there. Boo! Woof!

*(The **Bear** and the **Lion** get up and sniff at each other sociably.)*

Whoever heard of wild animals behaving like that?

*(Enter the **Monkey**.)*

Another one! . . . It's a zoo. Sit down, Monkey, sit down. Now, look here, my pets, here have I been working every day for a whole year and not one of you has even shown me the tip of his nose before. Are you out to make trouble for me now that I've finished my work? Come, you can't mean that, surely. *(He thinks it over.)* Unless . . . Oh! But that makes all the difference. Lord! Lord! *(Between his teeth.)* Not there as usual.

*(Enter the **Elephant**.)*

Get back there, Jumbo! No pushing out of turn.

*(The **Elephant** salutes him.)*

Good morning, old fellow. Now, if I understand you rightly, you want to come on board, eh?

(The animals move forward.)

Stop! I didn't say you could! . . . Well. All right, I'll let you come aboard. Yes, I don't see what I can . . . No, I don't see anything against it. *(He sighs deeply.)* So the time has come! All right. Up with you!

*(Enter the **Cow**, gambolling.)*

Gently there, gently . . . *(He taps the **Cow** on the rump.)* Wait a minute. Don't I know you? Aren't you that old cow from Mordecai's herd?

*(The **Cow** moos gaily.)*

Bless my soul! *(With feeling.)* And he picked on you! . . . *(To the **Bear**.)* Well, my friend, will you make up your mind?

*(The **Bear** sniffs the ground, but doesn't advance.)*

What's the matter, old boy? *(**Noah** puts on his spectacles and leans over the spot where the **Bear** is sniffing.)* What? Afraid of that insect? An ant! Ha, ha, ha! A bear afraid of an ant. Ha ha, ha! *(But suddenly he strikes his brow.)* Oh! but what a fool I am! Why, it's not an ant, it's *the* ant! It got here first, and I never saw it. Lord! What marvels there are on the threshold of this new life. It will take a stout heart, a steady hand, and a clear eye! I think my heart is right, but my eyes are dim . . . my hands are trembling . . . my feet are heavy . . . Ah, well, if You've chosen me, perhaps it's because I am, like her — the least wicked of the herd. Come, all aboard. Make yourselves at home.

(The animals go into the Ark.)

Straight ahead, across the deck! Down the stairway to the left. You'll find your cabins ready. They may look like cages, but they'll be open always. *(He turns towards the forest.)* Come on, all of you! Hurry, you lazybones, you slow-coaches, creepy crawlers; you who travel in herds and you who walk alone — mustangs, mastodons, jabberwocks and unicorns, cloven hoofs and crumpled horns! Hurry! Every one! Everyone! *(He catches his breath.)* Ah, ha! Here come the wolf and the lamb, side by side.

*(The **Wolf** and the **Lamb** enter and go into the Ark.)*

Here are the frog and the bull . . . The fox and the crow . . . And the birds! what are they waiting for? Come, my little ones. Come! Come!

(The singing of the birds begins.)

Look. The hare and the tortoise. Come on. Come on. Hurrah! The hare wins! Things are getting back to normal! Ah, this will be the golden age.

*(A great concert of birds. **Noah** falls on his knees. A pause. Then the **Tiger** enters behind **Noah**. He goes to **Noah** and taps him on the shoulder. The birds are suddenly still.)*

(Terrified.) Ooooo! *(He rises to flee.)* I know you wouldn't hurt me; it's just the surprise, you know. I'm not a bit afraid . . . *(His teeth are chattering.)* I'm not afraid a bit. It's not me. It's just that my feet have gone cold! It'll soon pass. Wait a minute! They are still cold.

*(The **Tiger** creeps towards him.)*

Perhaps, if I do this . . . *(He turns his back and covers his ears.)* Go on, get aboard! Hurry up.

*(The **Tiger**, with one bound, leaps aboard the Ark.)*

Are you still there?

(Roaring from the Ark.)

Good. *(**Noah** turns around and wipes his brow.)* Phew!

*(Off stage is heard the voice of a boy. It is **Japheth**.)*

Japheth   Whoo-hoo! Father!

Noah Ah, here come the children . . . Whoo-hoo!

Japheth *(nearer)* Whoo-hoo!

Noah Whoo-hoo!

Voice of Shem Look here, Japheth. We agreed; no running. Stick to the rules, or I won't play.

Japheth *(entering up R. He is seventeen)* I'm not running. Morning, Dad! *(He goes to* **Noah** *in great strides.)*

Shem *(entering up L. He is twenty-one)* You are running! Isn't he, Father?

Japheth *(throws himself into* **Noah's** *arms)* Home! I told you my way was shorter.

Shem If you're going to run the whole way . . . Hello, Father.

Noah *(embracing them both)* Good morning, children. You both win; Japheth got here first, but he cheated a little. Well, my big sons, did you have much difficulty finding where I was?

Japheth Hoho, Dad! So this is where you've been coming every day. Come on, tell us about it.

Noah Just a minute.
(Enter **Ham** *L. He is nineteen.)*

Shem
Japheth } We beat you!

Ham All right, all right.

Shem
Japheth } We won!

Ham All right! *(He goes to* **Noah**.*)* Good morning, Father.

Noah *(embracing him)* Hello, Ham, my boy. *(To the three of them.)* Where is your mother?

Ham She's coming.

Noah One of you might have waited for her.

*(**Ham** wanders over to the Ark.)*

Japheth She didn't want us to. She said she'd get along better alone. Then she can puff as much as she likes.

Noah   You can both go back some of the way and meet her.

Shem   *(lying on the ground)* Aw, Father, it's so hot.

Japheth   Come on, we'll take it slowly.

Shem   *(getting up)* Oh, what a bore!

(They go toward the L.)

Japheth   *(pointing to the Ark)* New house?

Noah   Ssshh!

Japheth   It's nice.

Noah   Isn't it?

*(**Shem** and **Japheth** go out down L. **Ham** is examining the Ark, his hands behind his back. **Noah** goes to him and takes his arm.)*

Well, son what do you think of it?

Ham   That?

Noah   Why, yes.

Ham   What is it?

Noah   Can't you guess? Is it such a funny shape?

Ham   Hm! It's hard to say. Come on, Father, what is it exactly?

Noah   It's . . . well, it's made of cypress. It's all cypress. And it's . . . it's coated with pitch, inside and out.

Ham   Like a boat.

Noah   Like a . . . yes. Hm! And it's three hundred cubits long and fifty cubits wide and thirty cubits high . . .

Ham   But that's ten times too big for us.

Noah   It's . . . yes it's pretty big. But does it . . . look like *anything*?

Ham   It's not bad . . . not bad, but why build a house like a boat?

Noah   Ah! It does look like a . . .?

Ham   Exactly.

Noah   Listen. *(His tone changes.)* Who knows what will happen? Suppose there was a great flood . . .

Ham   *(laughing)* Here?

Noah   A . . . tidal wave . . .

Ham   In this part of the world?

Noah   A deluge . . .

(A noise is heard off.)

*(To **Ham**.)* Ssshh!

*(Enter **Shem** and **Japheth**, carrying their **Mother** on their arms and singing: 'Here is Mamma. Look at Mamma. See who is bringing in darling Mamma.')*

Shem ⎫
        ⎬   Here is Mamma.
Japheth ⎭   Look at Mamma.
                See who is bringing in darling Mamma.

*(**Noah** begins to laugh. **Shem** and **Japheth** seat **Mamma** on the grass and dance around her.)*

Ham   Oh, don't make such a row!

Noah   Good morning, old lady, good morning! *(He kisses her.)*

Mamma   *(panting)* Phew! Phew!

Noah   Tired, eh?

Mamma   It's so terribly hot. *(To **Japheth**.)* Oh, did you lock the door carefully?

Japheth   Why . . . er . . . yes.

Mamma   You didn't at all.

Japheth   I did, but . . . I think I left the key in the lock.

Mamma   We must get it out at once. Run back to the house —

Japheth   Oh, I say look here! . . .

Mamma   Go on, run!

Noah   No, you stay here! *(To **Mamma**.)* I'm sorry, Mother, but it's no use getting the key.

Mamma   No use! . . . What, with neighbours like ours?

Noah   Well . . . I had a nice little speech in my head explaining everything, but now I don't know quite how to tell you . . . My dear wife, my darling children, we're never going back to our house . . . There!

(A short pause.)

The Three Boys What?

Mamma For months I've felt that there was something worrying you. Why don't you tell me about it? You know I always understand.

Ham Father always likes a mystery.

Noah Don't be so silly.

Ham All right, but you must admit that we might have been consulted. People don't build houses out in the middle of a forest miles from everybody, and everything. Why, just to get provisions it'll take two hours, there and back.

Noah Be quiet.

Ham Suppose mother forgets the bread . . . and that has been known to happen . . .

Noah *(laughing bitterly)* Bread! Ha, ha, ha! bread . . .

Ham We'll need it, won't we? Aren't we going to eat any more?

Noah Be quiet, do you hear? Quiet!

Mamma Now stop it, both of you, stop it! All right, dear, we're not going home any more. That's that. You've told us the worst, I suppose.

Japheth And I don't see that it's so terrible. This house looks much nicer than the old one. Doesn't it, Shem?

Shem *(practically asleep)* Hmmmm?

Japheth You see, he isn't losing any sleep over it.

*(**Japheth** and **Mamma** have a good laugh.)*

Noah How sweet of you! How sweet of you both to take it like this.

Mamma We are very fond of you, that's all. It isn't hard to be fond of someone like you. Now finish your story and we'll go and see our new house.

Noah *(in a low voice)* It isn't a house.

Japheth
Mamma } What?

Japheth *(nudging **Shem**)*. Listen to this, you.

Noah   It's not a house.

Shem   What is it?

Noah   It's a ship.

Mamma
The Boys } A what?

Noah   A ship.

Japheth   Splendid!

Ham   Nonsense!

Shem   *(sitting up)* Honest Injun?

Mamma   A ship!

Japheth   Didn't I tell you? Shem, what did I tell you? It's a boat.

Shem   Can we go on board?

Noah   Not without me. Admire it from here.

Ham   That's right. Wait.

(The two boys go behind the Ark.)

Shem   What shall we call it?

Mamma   A ship.

Ham   What on earth for?

Noah   Well . . . er . . . for going sailing.

Ham   Sailing! But on what?

Noah   God will provide, my son.

Ham   Oh, come now, father. Let's be serious.

Noah   We're going sailing. Yes . . . we're going on a little trip.

Mamma   But you hate trips.

Noah   Oh no, no! One can change one's mind sometimes, you know.

We'll be nice and quiet, all by ourselves. We won't see another soul. People are pretty unbearable nowadays, don't you think? Wicked! Coarse! Hateful! A bit of solitude with nothing but sea and sky will do us a world of good, it will give us new ideas. And when we get back . . . *(In a low voice.)* When we get back . . .

Ham   But, my dear father, here we are living in the middle of such a terrible drought that we've almost forgotten what water's like, hundreds of miles from the sea, with every stream and river as dry as a bone, and you, who've been a farmer all your life, suddenly choose this moment to want to be a sailor.

Noah   No, it isn't that, a bit. I don't feel that at all.

Mamma   *(tenderly)* Tell us, Noah. There's something on your mind, I'm sure. Tell us about it.

Ham   Yes, for heaven's sake, tell us.

Voice of Japheth   *(off stage)* Why, this is wonderful!

Voice of Shem   You bet it is. This is great!

Noah   Come on, let's go and join them *(He helps* **Mamma** *to her feet.)* It will do us good to hear them laugh.

Ham   But, father . . .

Japheth   *(appearing R., beaming)* Papa! What's that gadget with the rope . . .!

Noah   Gadget? Rope! Which one? There are plenty of gadgets and ropes.

Japheth   The one with the two pulleys in front; a big one and a little one, for lifting machinery.

Noah   Ah, yes.

Japheth   Well, it's a stroke of genius! Come and see it, Ham.

Ham   All right! What's the hurry?

Japheth   You're a genius, father.

Shem   *(appearing)* Japheth, come and see the sliding panel. Father, you're an ace! Mother, your husband's an ace!

Mamma   I don't doubt it for a minute.

Japheth   But, father, how did you ever invent it?

Noah   I'll tell you. Have you ever noticed that when a wood-cutter wants to lift a tree-trunk . . . the way he rolls up his rope . . .

(They go out up R.)

Ham   *(following them)* Crazy!

(Their voices die away.)

*(Enter from back, three girls: **Ada, Sella** and **Naomi**.)*

Ada   Come, girls, follow the cat. Don't lose it. I feel we must follow the cat.

Sella   And *I* think it's getting us lost. We've never been so far into the forest.

Naomi   Besides, we've lost it.

Ada   Then we must look for it. We've got to find it. Hunt for it, sisters, hunt for it! *(She calls.)* Kitty! Kitty!

Sella
Naomi } Kitty, Kitty, Kitty!

(They make the little lip-noise which calls cats.)

Ada   There it is. Look at its little white tail sliding through the grass. Come on, come on!

Naomi   I can't go any further. It's so hot!

(They see the Ark.)

Ada   Look! A woodcutter's house.

Sella   Huh. What a funny-looking house.

Naomi   Ada, I'm afraid you've led us into some kind of danger.

Ada   We must go into that house.

Sella   *(frightened)* Oh, no!

Naomi   No, no!

Sella   Please, let's go back!

Naomi   Yes! Yes, let's try to find the road back to the village.

*(**Mrs Noah's** voice off, 'Kitty, Kitty'.)*

Ada   Be quiet. Listen.

Voice of Mamma   Oh, look! The cat! Noah! Noah! Look at the cat!

Japheth   Kitty!

Noah   Kitty!

Shem   Well, if it isn't dear old Kitty!

Ada   What did I tell you? *(She calls.)* Mrs Noah!

The Three Girls   Mrs Noah.

*(**Mamma** enters up **R**.)*

Mamma   What's this? You here, my pretties? *(She calls off stage.)* Shem! Ham! Japheth! Come and see your friends. *(To the girls.)* What brought you here?

Ada   *(wrapping her arms about **Mamma's** neck)* Oh, Mrs Noah. Dear Mrs Noah!

Mamma   There, there. What's the matter?

Sella   She's been excited all morning.

(Three boys enter down R.)

Naomi   Yes. She couldn't stay still. She burst into tears for no reason at all.

Sella   She never stopped talking about you.

Naomi   She wanted to go to your house. She wanted to see you. She insisted on seeing you.

Ada   Dear Mrs Noah! *(To her sisters.)* We've just escaped a great danger.

Noah   *(enters above Ark)* How do you know, little one?

Ade   I . . . I feel it. *(She goes and kneels before **Noah**.)* I'm *sure* of it.

*(**Noah** lifts her up, gazes at her, presses her to him, and raises his eyes to heaven. A short silence.)*

The Three Boys   *(in a low voice, but joyously)* Good morning!

Sella }
Naomi } Good morning!

Japheth Are you sailing with us?

Sella and Naomi What?

Shem You know, you'd make pretty little cabin-boys.

Sella }
Naomi } Pretty . . . *What?*

Ham If we have to draw lots to see who's to be eaten, I hope the lot falls on Naomi. She's so nice and brown. I'll take a wing, please.

(**Mamma** *and the boys laugh.*)

Naomi What are you talking about?

(*More laughter.*)

Noah   *(coming back to earth)* Yes, you have indeed escaped a great danger. *(A pause; then joyously.)* Why on earth didn't I think of it before? We have three lovely neighbours . . . Orphans if you please. They share our life with us. We say our prayers together. We talk across the fence. And I — I forgot all about them! Now, isn't it lucky that . . . But how did you happen to meet the cat?

Ada   She was over in your house . . .

Mamma   Oh, you've been to our house?

Ada   Yes.

Sella   Yes. Do you know there were a lot of people waiting outside.

Noah   Aha.

Naomi   Oh, yes, a whole crowd. Men and women and children from the village. And some men from other villages, too. And they were all whispering and waving their arms.

Noah   Ah! We were just in time! . . . Go on.

Sella   All of a sudden Ada cried out, 'Come with me.'

Naomi   She took each of us by the hand and led us out of doors.

Sella   We went through the crowd —

Noami   We found ourselves at your gate.

Ada   I pulled away a man who was listening at the door. I went in —

Mamma   Japheth, the key!

Ada   Nobody was there.

Sella   Except the cat.

Ada   Except the cat. She rubbed herself against my legs and meowed enough to break your heart.

Mamma   Poor Kitty!

Ada   We came out again . . .

Sella   That is, we wanted to get out but the crowd was so thick —

Naomi   It was like a wall of faces across the door . . .

Japheth   Meow!

Sella   She arched her back —

Naomi   She spat like mad —

Ada   And the crowd backed away.

(The three boys laugh.)

Ada   So we went through. We followed the cat and she led us into the forest.

The Boys   Ah!

Sella   Every now and then she turned around to see if we were following.

The Boys   Oh!

Naomi   We lost her!

The Boys   Och!

Ada   We found her again!

The Boys   Whee!

Ada
Sella   } And here we are!
Naomi

The Boys   Hurray!

(General embraces.)

Ham   *(To **Noah**.)* Now, are you going to explain?

Noah   *(his voice vibrating)* Yes!

All   Ah!

Noah   I'll tell you everything. It's a great secret, a terrible secret. It has been vexing my heart and preying on my mind for months . . . for a whole year . . . I had no right to trouble you with it before. But now . . . today . . .

Japheth   Sshh!

Noah   Eh!

Japheth   *(in a low voice)* Someone's hiding just over there!

All   Where?

Japheth   Sshh! There. *(He points off L.)* In the bushes.

(*Something whistles over the stage.*)

The Three Boys   An arrow!

Noah   Women to the back!

(**Mamma** *and the girls retreat toward the Ark.*)

(*Another whistling.*)

The Boys   Another!

Noah   To the ship!

(*All move toward the Ark. A shout off stage. Then a* **Man**, *a sort of hunter, with a savage face, runs in from the L., stops short, plants himself firmly, points a spear at* **Noah**.)

The Man   Stop! . . . Stop! . . . Stop! *(To the girls who are moving up the ladder.)* Well, you fillies, are you deaf? One move and I skewer the old boy to the wall.

Japheth   *(trying to drag his brothers)* Come on! Let's go for him!

Mamma   Don't move.

Man   *(to* **Japheth**.) If you are looking for trouble, cocky . . .

Noah   Steady, Japheth, steady. He'll kill you.

Man   You bet I will!

Mamma
The Children } Scoundrel! Ruffian!

Noah   Silence.

(*Mutterings from the Youngsters.*)

Now that's enough! *(To the* **Man**.) Don't keep on waving that thing about. Your arm will get tired.

Man   I seen you. I seen you! You sorcerer. Talking to the animals. Pinching a cow from Mordecai. Playing with bears and lions and tigers, not to mention elephants. I seen you! The whole village is going to know. I'll tell them. Sorcerer! Sorcerer!

The Three Boys   Stop it!

Man   It's none of your business. All you've got to do is keep your mouth shut. What's more, the animals are in there! *(He points to the Ark.)* I've seen 'em coming. That's where they are. . . in there!

*(**Mamma** and the **Youngsters** laugh. The **Man** rushes to the Ark and beats on it with his fist. Roaring from the animals.)*

Mamma
The Youngsters } *(frightened)* Oh!

Man   Hahaha! Who's laughing now? Ah, he looks gentle enough, but he's up to plenty of tricks behind your back! He's bad. He never could make anything with his hands before that. *(Pointing to Ark.)* He's a menace to the whole country.

Mamma   Be quiet.

Man   Listen, I'll tell you something. This drought that's been roasting us for three months, that nobody's never seen nothing like before, that'll knock us all dead with our mouths open this winter . . . that's him. He done it! He's the one that done it.

Noah   Are you sure you're quite all right in the head?

Man   You done it! There! We all got together! We took a vote. And we all voted alike — unanimous — that it's all your fault.

Noah   Oh, well, in that case . . .

Man   I seen you! You look up in the air like this. *(He imitates **Noah** says to me, 'Watch that old bird,' he says. 'He acts stupid but he knows all the tricks.' Everything that's gone wrong . . . he started it.

Mamma   Oh, Noah, if they think that, that's terrible!

Noah   Ssshh! Ssshh!

Man   I seen you! You look up in the air like this *(He imitates **Noah** praying.)* And straight away it gets hotter, and hotter. I seen you doing your abracadabra. And then the sky opens like an oven door, and the oven is white hot, and the ground where I was lying was like a gridiron.

Youngsters   *(in a low voice)* Oh!

Man   All right, now you got to pay for it. Yes, you've got to come with me. But I don't need the whole issue. The head'll do. *(He leaps towards* **Noah**.*)*

*(***Mamma*** *and the* ***Girls*** *scream. The* ***Boys*** *line up in front of* ***Noah***.*)*

Noah   You wretched creature! *(He steps in front of them all and smiles. A pause.)* This drought — *(He half turns toward his family.)* . . . He hoped it would make them see; that they'd say to themselves, 'It must be. It's a judgment from heaven.' I told them so myself, in every possible way. They laughed in my face. They spat on me. They threw stones at me.

Mamma
The Youngsters } Yes.

Noah   Didn't I tell them often enough?

Mamma
The Youngsters } Oh, yes.

Noah   I told them again and again, didn't I?

Mamma
The Youngsters } Oh yes, yes, yes.

Noah   *(turning towards the* ***Man***) Fool! To think they're all like you. Idle, greedy, thieving, wicked!

*(***Man*** *sneers*.*)*

And on top of that, sneering and sniggering at everything!

Man   Aw, you old fool. You old idiot.

Noah   *(walking up to him)* Tell me, my friend, can you swim?

Man   What?

Noah   I asked you if you could swim.

Man   Aw, come on! None of your tricks with me. I know you.

Noah   Once and for all, yes or no. Can you swim?

Man   Of course.

Noah   Can you swim for a long time?

Man   You bet!

Noah   You'll have to swim for a long time . . . So long that it might be better if you couldn't swim at all. Then it would be over sooner.

Man   Over?

Noah   Yes, over. That's what I said — finished.

Man   What's going to be finished?

Noah   Everything! You. Your friends. Your relations. The village. All the villages. This forest. All the forests, all the animals, all human beings in the water! Under the water! With your sins like stones around your neck.

Man   *(bending double)* Hahahahaha!

Noah   *(bending double too)* Hahahahahaha!

Man   Hahahahahaha!

Noah   It's going to rain. Rain! You hear what I say? . . . Rain!

*(The **Man**, the **Children**, and **Mamma** raise their eyes to the sky.)*

Man   Hahahahahaha!

Ham   *(to **Shem**, under his breath)* Has father got a touch of the sun? There's not a cloud in the sky!

Noah   Such rain as has never been before. Pouring, drenching, spouting rain. Water swirling, water roaring — hurricanes sweeping madly across the sky — tattered clouds streaming out like great black flags ripped by lightning. Fish will play in the trees. On the tops of mountains, where there were soaring eagles, there will be ravening sharks. And the bodies of the drowned with arms outstretched, rolling over and over, down and down and down. He told me.

Man   Who?

Noah   God.

Man   Who's that?

Noah   *God!*

Man   Oh, of course!

Noah   *(louder)* God.

Man Try again.

Noah *(very loud)* Almighty God!

*(**Mamma** and the **Children** drop to their knees.)*

Man Hahahaha! *(He stutters with glee.)* God! . . . *(He stops short. His hands go to his forehead.)*

(The light dims.)

Noah Splash! Did you feel that, my friend? You felt the first drop! Right on your forehead, between the eyes, as straight as a die. A perfect shot. *(Savagely.)*

*(**Mamma** and the children rise trembling.)*

Man Oh, you think so? Well, it was a bird — a sparrow.

Noah And that?

*(The **Man's** hand goes to the back of his neck.)*

I suppose that was a nightingale? And that?

*(The **Man's** hand covers his eyes.)*

A robin, maybe?

*(The **Man** stretches out his hands and quickly draws them in again.)*

And those. A brace of pigeons?

Mamma
The Children } Oh?

Noah Dance, my friend, dance!

*(And the **Man** dances as if he were trying to avoid a cloud of arrows.)*

Shoot, O Lord! Strike this vile target, pierce it through and through!

Mamma
The Children } *(every hand extended)* It's raining, raining, raining!

*(Pantomime of the **Children** seeking the rain with every gesture around the **Man** whose every gesture dodges the rain. The light is growing dim.)*

Noah Pierce the wicked eyes! The prying nose. Those ears. Seal up those lips and silence that blaspheming tongue. Pierce the hands that were never raised to You! The feet that strayed! The glutton's belly and his heart, split that accursed heart. Shoot, King of Archers, shoot!

*(The **Man** sinks down, still warding off the rain with both hands.)*

Man   Help! Help! It's burning . . .

(The light grows dimmer.)

Mamma   *(her hands stretched to the rain)* It's cool, cool like the evening breeze.

The Children *(their hands outstretched)* Like the evening breeze.

Mamma   Like the blue of the sky.

The Children   Like the blue of the sky.

Mamma   Like the laughter of angels.

The Children   The laughter of angels . . .

The Man   *(on his knees)* Help me! Help me! Help me! Help me!

(Thunder rolls.)

Noah   All aboard! Into the Ark, my good crew! Heavy weather to-night! Up into our home! Into the ship of God! You first, Mother, then you, Ada! now Sella! Naomi! Shem! Ham! Japheth! And we must sing, my children, come! all together, sing!

(A clap of thunder.)

*(The chorus is singing in unison. **Noah** goes up last. The storm rages. It is completely dark.)*

(The singing spreads through the Ark.)

END OF SCENE ONE

Questions

1   How does Noah treat the Bear?

2   How does Noah feel when the tiger taps him on the shoulder?

3   Why does Noah's family feel that a flood is most unlikely?

4   What were the girls doing when they came upon the Ark?

5   What kind of a man is Noah?

6   Why did the Man think that Noah was a sorcerer?

7   Why is the Man an evil person?

8   Why does Noah ask the Man whether he can swim?

9   How did God punish the evil people of Noah's time?

10   What are some of the problems you could expect if you tried to put *Noah* on stage?